TEAM MINISTRY

*A Guide to Spiritual Gifts
and Lay Involvement*

Larry Gilbert

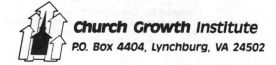

Church Growth Institute
P.O. Box 4404, Lynchburg, VA 24502

First Printing, January 1987
Second Printing, March 1988
Third Printing, March 1989
Fourth Printing, February 1990
Copyright © 1987 Church Growth Institute
TEAM Ministry is a registered trademark of Church Growth Institute
Printed in the United States of America
ISBN: 0-941005-003

TABLE OF CONTENTS

FOREWORD

I believe one of the key ingredients to building an effective growing church is spiritual gifts. The key phrase is "using people where they are usable." If every Christian were involved according to his spiritual gifts, he would be used in ministering where he is most usable. I find that growing churches cannot be disassociated from growing Christians. Therefore, when a person has found his gifts, knows the significance of his gifts and properly exercise his gifts, he will grow. As he grows (internal growth) then his church will grow (external growth).

I believe *TEAM Ministry* by Larry Gilbert is some of the best material that has been written on spiritual gifts. It will help to build a strong foundation in a local church. It will inspire leadership, motivate laymen and turn a church around.

TEAM Ministry is the result of ten years of study, research and observation of church ministries by Larry Gilbert. I have worked with him and we have had long discussions in the area of spiritual gifts. We have worked together on church growth projects such as *Friend Day, Tithing Is Christian* and *God Is Able* . . . . These programs were never just gimmicks or campaigns, they were built on church growth principles and the use of spiritual gifts.

I believe that Larry Gilbert understands the foundation of spiritual gifts for church growth. Therefore, this book will make a significant contribution for the reader to help him build a church to the glory of God.

> Dr. Elmer Towns
> Dean, B. R. Lakin School of Religion
> Liberty Universtiy
> Lynchburg, Virginia

PREFACE

"Go ye therefore, and teach all nations, baptizing them in the name of the Father, and of the Son, and of the Holy Ghost: teaching them to observe all things whatsoever I have commanded you: and, lo, I am with you alway, even unto the end of the world." (Matthew 28:19-20)

The Great Commission is the greatest command, given by the greatest Commander, to the greatest army, for the greatest task ever. Although many churches have argued it, debated it, denied it and ignored it, most have accepted it as their marching orders. Outreach, evangelism and soul-winning have become the very heartbeat of many churches. We have recognized this *task* and boldly set out to accomplish this seemingly unreachable goal. In fact, most aggressive churches' whole philosophy of ministry evolves from and revolves around the Great Commission, or the Great Task.

Unfortunately, some have forgotten that the God who assigned us this great *task* also assigned us the *means* to fulfill the task — *people*, men and women whom God has equipped to fulfill that task, men and women with God-given gifts — *spiritual gifts*.

The cry of the Christian has resembled the challenge of Sir Winston Churchill during World War II, "Give us the tools, and we will finish the job." The desire of most Christians and of most churches is that God would equip them for the task of carrying out the Great Commission. There is good news for those who have such a desire — God has already answered your prayer.

Spiritual gifts are God's tools and are created by God to fulfill the task. Methods and programs are man's tools, created by *man* to fulfill the task. Both are a necessity, yet many work apparently unaware of the instruments God created for this task.

It seems the church is constantly pushed to devise new plans, new and better organizations and new methods in order to enlarge our congregations and evangelize the present generation. Tragically though, such a philosophy rapidly loses sight of the individual by sinking him or her into the plans or organization. God's plans make much of the individual, far more than anything else God may use. *People are God's method. The church is looking for better methods; God is looking for better men and women who can help carry out His plan.*

The utilization of spiritual gifts already given to Christians by God is the most efficient way there is to build better churches. The future of the growing church is in the hands of the pastor who becomes "gift oriented", helping his people recognize their spiritual gifts, developing them and teaching them how to use their gifts, thus utilizing the "equipping of the saints" rather than the programs of the church to do the job.

I am not belittling church programs. In fact, this book is part of a program. My whole ministry is for the purpose of developing new church programs. Programs are a necessity, but programs are to complement God-gifted Christians — not replace them.

This book introduces a philosophy of ministry — a philosophy that revolves around people, not around the task — a philosophy I call *TEAM MINISTRY.* In order to express the basis for this philosophy, this book centers on four themes:

(1) God has given the Great Commission to the church and has equipped the body to fulfill it collectively through a gifted, informed, understanding and cooperating TEAM.

(2) The individual believer can discover and understand his spiritual gifts, thus finding his place on that TEAM.

(3) Gifts relate to and are fundamental to the church, to the believer, to the ministry, and to both quantitative and qualitative church growth.

(4) The lack of recognition, understanding and implementation of spiritual gifts are the missing ingredients to equipping, preparing and motivating the layman to do the work of the ministry.

This book is an attempt to properly identify that God-gifted workforce and bring it together with the God-given task for the purpose of *reaching* a lost world and *teaching* it to grow, become involved with the ministry and mature into the image of Christ — during this generation.

NOW WHAT?

At the close of every chapter (except six, seven and eight, which are combined) there is added a section titled *NOW WHAT*. It is a conclusion drawn from the material presented in the chapter. It is not enough just to learn the definitions, characteristics and principles of spiritual gifts and not put them into practice in daily living and service for God. Therefore, I draw a conclusion and explain how to make a personal and practical application of that chapter in daily living

STOP

Before you go any further *please* answer these 2 questions.

The answers to these questions will help you recognize your spiritual gift. I have found that if you answer the questions before being influenced, you will be able to distinguish your gift with less confusion. So, please answer the questions, now, before you go on.

We will refer back to them in Chapter Twelve.

1. If you had no restrictions and were free to get involved in any spiritual activity or task, what would you like to do?

_____

_____

_____

_____

2. What my church needs is. . .

_____

_____

_____

SECTION ONE

THE RELATIONSHIPS OF SPIRITUAL GIFTS

CHAPTER ONE

SPIRITUAL GIFTS AND THEIR RELATIONSHIP TO LEADERSHIP

In my younger years, I was the owner of an electric sign business. Not only did I learn much about leadership by managing my company through the ups and downs of business, but because of the type of business it was, I had the opportunity to be closely associated with and observe many other businessmen. All of my customers were business people. Over the years, I watched many businesses come and go. In fact, I watched as ninety percent of these new businesses failed within their first five years. The reason they failed was due to their owners' inability to lead and manage. They failed to manage the resources available to them, they failed to manage their time and money, and most importantly, they failed to lead and manage the people they had gathered to help them carry out their goals.

On the other side of the spectrum, most businesses that do succeed will never fulfill the dream their owner and founders envisioned for them. Again, the lack of ability to lead and manage puts uncontrolled limitations on these business people. Through my years of self-employment and the opportunity to work with and evaluate literally hundreds of businesses, I had determined that success in business can be reduced to one simple leadership principle *the size of every business is regulated by the leadership capacity of its owner.*

After being called into the ministry and working in churches, I, like many Christian leaders, ignored the principles that I had learned in secular business. My logic was that anything secular could not be applicable for the church. However, I was quick to realize that these principles are just as valid in the church as they are in any business. In fact, I soon revised my success principle to read, *the size of every church is regulated by the leadership capacity of its pastor,* and began to formulate a distinctive parallel between leadership in business and leadership in the church. I realized that leadership was not something that started at the low end of the spectrum and grew at a steady incline until it reached its maximum. Leadership is developed on plateaus. For a businessman or a pastor to expand his capacity in leadership, he must grow within these plateaus.

I have developed a chart that clarifies the three plateaus of leadership in business and parallels them with the three plateaus of leadership in the church. I will explain these plateaus and their relationship to spiritual gifts in this chapter.

The Three Plateaus of Leadership	
BUSINESS	**CHURCH**
1. Owner/Operator	Church-Planter
2. Manager	Ephesians 4 Pastor
3. Executive	Multistaffed Pastor

Plateau 1. In business this first plateau of leadership is called the *owner/operator*. This individual goes into business for himself and does everything that needs to be done in the business. He owns it and operates it. He makes the product, does all the office functions, sweeps the floors, scrubs the hoppers—does whatever needs to be done. The owner/operator is usually the entrepreneur—the person who is willing to go out on the limb and take all the risks.

In the church the first plateau is called the *church-planter*. The church-planter starts a church or takes over a small church and does basically the same thing as the owner/operator. He takes care of business, prepares and preaches the sermons, is the Sunday School superintendent and a Sunday School teacher. Basically, just like the business owner/operator, the church-planter does *everything* that has to be done in the church.

Plateau 2. Plateau number two is where the businessman and pastor realize they can no longer do it *all* themselves. Their time is consumed with the business or the church. They no longer have time for family or any activities other than business. Even then they are not able to get all the work done that is required. They cannot work 28 hours a day, and soon come to the conclusion that if their business or ministry is going to prosper, they need help. They must delegate these tasks to others.

However, the businessman, instead of going to plateau 2, mistakenly goes the route of what I call the *proprietor*. He decides to hire people to help him. The pastor goes the route of the *multistaffed pastor (prematurely)*. After all, if you are going to delegate you must have someone to delegate to.

But the problem is that neither the proprietor nor the pastor have learned to delegate. When the proprietor hires a helper, he is just that—a helper. The boss still drives the truck; the helper goes along to hand him the tools. The boss still does the paperwork; the helper assists with clerical functions. What the proprietor has done is not delegate any major responsibilities, only given some distasteful duties such as cleaning the hopper, stocking the shelves, or simply *helping* with jobs.

If the businessman does not grow in his leadership ability and stays right there in this relationship with his one, two, or three helpers, the business' growth is hindered, because growth still directly revolves around the function of the owner.

Meanwhile the pastor who has now stepped into a premature multi-staffed position is doing the same thing. He has a helper who does some of the menial tasks. But now that there are two of them, he wonders why they cannot get twice as much done as before. If the pastor goes this route at this stage of the game, he too has locked his church out of growth. He ruins the potential of growing because he missed the *necessary* second plateau.

They have both taken what appears to be the natural second step, but it is not. It is a trap and most step into it by default.

The next step for the businessman should have been to become a *manager*. The manager hires people to work *for* him.

Plateau 2 for the pastor should have been to become an *Ephesians 4 Pastor*. Instead of hiring staff like the businessman, the *Ephesians 4 Pastor* takes advantage of the work force he already has—his laypeople. He trains them to utilize their gifts. When he does this he has all the work force he needs. When he cannot keep up with that any longer, *then* he should hire a staff.

The *Ephesians 4 Pastor* leads. He learns how to work with people. He develops a staff of laypeople. It is not always necessary to hire someone outside the church when you have laypeople who can handle the job.

In order to be an *Ephesians 4 Pastor*, the pastor must do what is necessary to perfect or equip the saints so they can do the work of the ministry. The bottom line is that as the membership does the work of the ministry, they edify the body of Christ.

By going from the owner/operator or church-planter stage right into the multistaffed position, the pastor does not develop a biblical work force. He only develops a staff that will do the work of the ministry like he did. This is where Ephesians 4 comes in, because it talks about spiritual gifts. In fact the only time the term *pastor* is used in Scripture is in Ephesians 4, where the passage mentions certain gifts, including pastor/teacher. "And he gave some, apostles; and some, prophets; and some evangelists; and some, pastors and teachers; For the perfecting of the saints, for the work of the ministry, for the edifying of the body of Christ" (Eph. 4:11-12).

There are two schools of thought regarding the interpretation of this Scripture. One interpretation is that the prophets, evangelists, and pastor/ teachers are given to the church to do three things:

1. perfect (equip) the saints
2. do the work of the ministry
3. edify (build up) the body of Christ

Coming from that interpretation, the pastor starts his church and becomes the owner/operator who does everything. He perfects the saints, does the work of the ministry, and edifies the body of Christ. He eventually needs help so he does the logical thing—hires more staff. As he expands his staff he sees himself as having a staff who perfects the saints, does the work of the ministry, and edifies the body of Christ. He has expanded the breadth of his ministry, but not the depth.

Interpretation number two, which the author holds to, is that the pastor was given for the perfecting of the saints (no comma, the comma was not there in the original and most scholars agree that it does not belong) for the work of the ministry. He is perfecting the saints, building them up, for the work of the ministry for the edifying of the body of Christ. Or in other words, "For the perfecting of the saints *so they can do* the work of the ministry." The pastor's job is not to do the work of the ministry. It is not to lead a staff to do the work of the ministry. It is to equip, train the saints (laypeople) so they can do the work of the ministry.

What is the *Ephesians 4 Pastor*? An *Ephesians 4 Pastor* is a *steward of the gifts, talents, and abilities of those entrusted to his care.* A true *Ephesians 4 Pastor* says, "I am not here to do the work of the ministry. I am here to equip my people, to build them up, train them, educate them so they can do the work of the ministry." He leads his people.

A good leader learns to be a good steward of all the resources available to him. The pastor's number one resource is all of the spiritual gifts that God has given to His people. God has given these gifts with the full intention that they be used in the church to do the work of the ministry. The *Ephesians 4 Pastor's* job is to develop the spiritual gifts of others and provide areas of service so they can exercise those gifts.

If the laypeople do not do the work of the ministry, it won't get done, because the pastor was not called to do the work of the ministry. He was called to lead the laypeople. If he cannot lead them to do it, then he is failing his calling. No one person can do it all. A pastor who cannot get the people to do the work, and tries to do it all himself, is like a mother who says, "Well, I can't get the kids to clean their rooms, so I will let them go out and play so they will be out of my way while I do it." She is wrong. If her job is to train her children so they will one day be responsible adults, then she cannot clean their rooms for them and let them play. Somewhere along the line she has to teach them how to do it. The same thing applies with the pastor.

The exception to that is that the pastor must grow through each plateau, starting with the owner/operator or church-planter. Just as Paul tells Timothy to "do the work of an evangelist," so must the pastor do it all in the beginning. Timothy was in a small, young church. He had to do everything. But a study of Timothy determines that he did not have the gift of evangelist. However, in getting started, Timothy had to do everything, just like the businessman or the new pastor has to do today.

As the church grows the pastor obviously needs more help. He should avoid defaulting into the premature multistaffed pastor and hiring staff. Instead he should become an *Ephesians 4 Pastor* and draw help from his congregation. If he hires more staff at this point he is eternally sending his church in the wrong direction. He would be training his staff to do the same thing he is doing—the work of the ministry. At best he is building a "spectator" church.

The time will come when he alone cannot train and keep all these laypeople involved. He will eventually have to become a multistaffed pastor. If he works with his laypeople and trains them to minister first, when he starts his staff they will be going in the right direction. The staff will continue what he started in the beginning—training and leading the laypeople to do the work of the ministry.

Plateau 3. The next stage is the true *multistaffed pastor*. In business he is the *executive*. Basically the executive's job is the same as the manager's in that he manages people. He studies, analyzes, gives direction, and motivates. He manages his organization by managing his managers, then his managers manage the work force. The difference between the manager and the executive is that a manager delegates the task but maintains the responsibility for the task. For example a manager tells an employee, "I want you to do this, this, and that, then I want to look it over when you are finished." He gives this person the task to do. The *responsibility* to get this job done remains on the shoulders of the manager. He does not actually do the task, but he oversees it while maintaining the responsibility.

On the other hand the *executive* delegates the responsibility. "Now manager, this is your job to get it done. You will be responsible for this area." The big difference between the function of executive and manager is that one delegates the responsibility along with the task while the other delegates the task and keeps the responsibility.

On the church side, we have the *multistaffed pastor*. He should delegate responsibility to his staff. The staff should lead the work force—the laity. When the pastor says, "Staff, here is what we need to do," he wants them to see that it gets done; to accept responsibility to delegate the task to the layworkers. For the pastor to learn to delegate properly, he needs to learn to delegate through his work force, his laity, *before* he can delegate to and train his multistaff. Whoever he delegates to becomes an extension of his pastoral ministry.

Benefits to the *Ephesians 4 Pastor*. The benefits of growing through each plateau in the proper order and becoming an *Ephesians 4 Pastor* include fulfillment and excitement of laypeople and building of churches. The church is using God's methodology by using the gifts He has given each person. If the pastor first utilizes the laity, then adds staff as necessary, the church will continue to grow in like manner. The people will be fulfilled and will all be involved in the work of the ministry. The church will not become stagnant, with only the leaders trying to do everything that needs to be done.

A benefit to the pastor is that as he understands his own spiritual gifts in light of their relationship to other areas of his ministry, he will better understand his own role and leadership style and will understand which plateau he is on. Is he locking himself into a premature multiple staff, or will he be the church-planter all his life? He must grow through one plateau to get to the next. He cannot successfully go from the church-planter straight to a multiple staff.

TEAM Ministry is a proven method to help the *Ephesians 4 Pastor* be successful. With *TEAM Ministry*, each member, including the leadership, learns his gift; understands where it fits into the established program of church ministry; understands his gift is part of a TEAM effort with the rest of the body; and is trained to develop the manifestation of the gift, which is the ministry of the gift. Any *Ephesians 4 Pastor* can experience similar results.

CHAPTER ONE

REVIEW QUESTIONS:

1. What are the three plateaus of leadership?

2. What is an *Ephesians 4 Pastor* and how does he interpret Ephesians 4:11-12?

3. How will the church benefit from the leadership of an *Ephesians 4 Pastor* and what are the benefits to the pastor himself?

DISCUSSION QUESTIONS:

1. Compare the plateaus of leadership to your ministry. What areas do you recognize that you could improve in your own life and ministry?

2. Do you feel there are people in your church who would be more involved if they knew their spiritual gifts and how to use them?

3. What could be done in your church if every member knew his spiritual gift? How many members do you think know their gifts?

CHAPTER TWO

SPIRITUAL GIFTS AND THEIR RELATIONSHIP TO CHRISTIANITY

The Gospel Herald once published a story about a man who had climbed to the top of his field and was relatively well-known in his country. It had been a long struggle and he had suffered many hardships and often ridicule as he made his way up the ladder of success. One day he sat contemplating his past and how he had made it to the top. He thought of all the influences and the people who had an impact on his life. He thought of his deceased parents and all their years of labor and love. He thought too of his wife and her patience and sacrifice. His children were now grown, and they had made such an impact on his life and maturity through the years.

Finally, his thoughts wandered to the one event and one person who had influenced him to success more than all of these people and all the other events put together. He did not know the name of the man and the words only made one sentence, but they had such an impact on his thinking that he was never the same again.

One summer afternoon, at a lake where he often swam with his friends, he was swimming alone. For some unknown reason, he suffered some physical problem and could swim no farther. He struggled for his life and was about to go under for the last time when he felt a man's strong arm lifting him from the water and taking him ashore. The boy never actually saw his rescuer's face and he could not recognize the voice. After making sure everything was well, the man left. As he did, the boy said, "Thank you, sir, for saving my life." The man replied, "You're welcome, son. See to it that you are worth saving."

So it is with the Christian. God has saved us and now says, "See to it that you are worth saving." The best part is that He gave us a way to see that we are "worth saving" — spiritual gifts to do His work and the power of the Holy Spirit for using those gifts.

"I could never get in front of a group of people and speak or go door to door, talking to people about their souls. Why, God hasn't given me any spiritual gifts. Maybe I'm just not spiritual enough for Him to trust me with any," is the cry of many Christians. If that were true, you would have no worth to God. But He must receive glory from our lives. In His providence He has provided a way for us to be "worth saving".

Every True Christian Has Spiritual Gifts

God gives *every believer* at least one spiritual gift at the time of the New Birth. Yet many live much or all of the Christian life without realizing that fact or the impact of such a truth.

The fact that every Christian receives at least one of the spiritual gifts is evident from the Scriptures. "For I say, through the grace given to me, to *every man* that is among you, not to think of himself more highly than he ought to think; but think soberly, according as God hath dealt to *every man* the measure of faith" (Romans 12:3). "But *every man* hath his proper gift of God, one after this manner, and another after that" (I Corinthians 7:7). "But the manifestation of the Spirit is given to *every man* to profit withal" (I Corinthians 12:7). "...dividing to *every man* severally as He will" (I Corinthians 12:11). "But unto *every one* of us is given grace according to the measure of the gift of Christ" (Ephesians 4:7). "As *every man* hath received the gift, even so minister the same one to another, as good stewards of the manifold grace of God" (I Peter 4:10).

It is clear from the context of these passages that God is talking about the Christian when He says, "every man" or "every one". In I Corinthians 12:29, Paul asks, "Are all apostles? Are all prophets? Are all teachers? Are all workers of miracles?" The obvious answer to Paul's series of questions is, "No"; therefore, we must conclude that all Christians have at least one spiritual gift and no Christian has them all.

It also seems that you receive this gift at the very moment of your salvation conversion, along with the Holy Spirit, the Enabler Who empowers us to use those gifts effectively. William McRae writes, "They (the gifts) are given to every individual believer. This seems to demand that it be at conversion. If it were subsequent to salvation, some may have a gift and others may not have a gift. Paul and Peter indicate that everyone to whom they are writing has a gift, not that some have one and that others will receive one."

"What about II Timothy 1:6 and I Timothy 4:14?" They seem to indicate that one receives his gift by the laying on of hands. This seems to be a special case because Timothy was to be an apostolic delegate with great authority. That his authority came through the apostle Paul is witnessed by the laying on of Paul's hands (II Timothy 1:6).

Again McRae writes, "In I Timothy 4:14 it was 'with the laying on of the hands by the presbytery.' The prophecy to Paul that Timothy should have a certain gift was followed by Paul's laying his hands on Timothy to bestow that gift on him. This gift was then recognized by the elders who were associated with Paul in this matter."[1]

Some Christians, in an attempt to humble themselves, deny that God would give them a gift. To that statement comes the reply, "Humility is the correct evaluation of your abilities and disabilities and living in the light of it. Humility is not a matter of denying one's God-given ability and potential, but of recognizing its presence, developing it and being thankful for it."

Every Christian Woman Has Spiritual Gifts

Throughout this material I use the terms he, him, his, himself in their generic sense only. Every gift and principle that pertains to men also pertains to women as well.

In fact, in this age of emphasis upon the woman's place in society and in particular, Christianity, it would be well to notice that there are two extremes in position concerning a woman's place in the ministry of God. The one extreme is to say the only place a woman can serve the Lord is to work in the nursery or the kitchen at a church fellowship meeting. The other extreme is to say a woman could serve as Pastor. Both are extreme and ignore the Biblical instruction for a woman to use her spiritual gift. The Bible is explicit in reference to some principles relating to women's leadership in the church. That teaching leaves room for the woman to exercise her spiritual gift without violating God's directives. When God gave a Christian woman her spiritual gift, He gave her a place in the church to use that gift.

Spiritual Gifts Declare The Presence Of The Holy Spirit

The Scriptures quoted earlier emphasize that the Christian is to use the gift to minister to others and that the power to use those gifts comes from the Holy Spirit. In fact, I Corinthians 12:7 would seem to indicate that the spiritual gift is one of the manifestations, or indicators, of the Holy Spirit's presence in the life of the believer. Galatians 5:22-23 tell us about the fruit of the Spirit, which are behavior patterns that result from the presence of the Holy Spirit in the believer. On the other hand, the references which tell about the spiritual gifts are referring to capacities given for service for Christ in the life of the believer. Fruit of the Spirit deals with attitude, gifts of the Spirit deal with action in service. Both are indications that the Holy Spirit is present in a person's life.

Spiritual gifts should not be confused with the fruit of the Holy Spirit. Bobby Clinton offers the following comparison in his book on spiritual gifts.

Gifts of the Spirit	Fruit of the Spirit
*Related primarily to the collective body of believers	*Related primarily to the individual believers in the body
*Related to ministry	*Related to character
*May be classified as to order of importance	*All are essential
*May be exercised in such a manner as to offend others and cause discord and division to the body	*Can never be misused
*No single believer receives all the gifts	*Every believer may bear all the fruits all the time
*No gift can be demanded of all believers	*All of us can be commanded to manifest the fruits

"The scriptural ideal seems to be the exercise of the gifts of the Spirit at the same time." Clinton goes on to indicate that both gifts and fruit of the Spirit are confirmation of the presence of the Holy Spirit in a life. Maturity is primarily indicated by Christlikeness as seen in the fruit of the Spirit and may not include the presence of the gifts or the exercise of the gifts.[2]

Spiritual gifts are not rewards. Gifts are given without regard to any degree of commitment. They are given by God's grace, not our faithfulness. They have nothing to do with how spiritual a person is. In I Corinthians 1:7, Paul says to the Corinthians, "ye come behind in no gift." Yet, we know the Corinthians were very unspiritual and immature.

Spiritual gifts are not to be confused with natural talent. You are given natural talents at your natural birth and spiritual talents (spiritual gifts) at your spiritual birth. Your responsibility as a Christian is to use both in service to glorify God.

Talents are available to the lost. Talents operate on a physical and social level. Talents alone cannot do God's work. Talents are not the primary channel God chose through which the Holy Spirit is to work.

A spiritual gift is not a place of service. Think *pastor-teacher* and you automatically think of the man behind the pulpit. Think *evangelist* and you think of the traveling preacher. These are not always true, although most of the time people with these gifts do hold these positions. The problem comes with our modern-day terminology. This will be made clearer as we study the individual gifts.

A spiritual gift is not an age-group ministry. Charles Ryrie writes, "There is no gift of young people's work or children's work. If there were, then there would be a gift of old people's work — a gift which the author has never heard anyone claim to have. Children, young and old adults all need the benefit from the exercise of gifts of pastor, teacher, etc."[3]

A spiritual gift is not a specialty of ministry. Again, Ryrie writes, "There is no gift of writing or Christian education named in the Scripture. The gift of teaching which is named, for instance, may be exercised through the education program of the church."[4] Music and athletics can also be put into this category. Teaching, exhortation and showing mercy can be exercised through the talents of music and athletics.

Spiritual Gifts And The Trinity

Use of the spiritual gifts is often misunderstood because of the misunderstanding of the source and the function of the gifts. Consider the following verses in I Corinthians 12:

vs. 4 "Now there are diversities of *gifts*, but the same *Spirit*."

vs. 5 "And there are differences of *administrations*, but the same *Lord*."

vs. 6 "And there are diversities of *operations*, but it is the same *God* which worketh all in all."

Addressing these verses, the *Liberty Commentary* states, "Paul is not necessarily classifying the gifts into three categories, but their relationship to the Spirit...Lord...God. They are the gifts given by the Spirit, used in ministry by the Son and energized by the Father."[5]

Although we think of spiritual gifts as coming only from the Holy Spirit, these verses show us that the function of spiritual gifts involves all three persons of the Trinity.

vs. 4 God the *Holy Spirit* gives the *gifts*.

vs. 5 God the *Son* places you in the *ministry*.

vs. 6 God the *Father* gives the *results*.

In his book, *Gifts of the Spirit*, Kenneth Cain Kinghorn offers the following explanation by using the gift of teaching as an example.

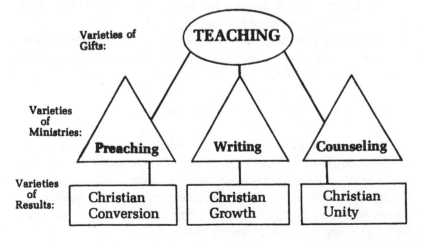

Varieties of Gifts: TEACHING

Varieties of Ministries: Preaching   Writing   Counseling

Varieties of Results: Christian Conversion   Christian Growth   Christian Unity

"Spiritual gifts express themselves through various ministries which, in turn, accomplish a variety of results. Let's illustrate it this way:

"Suppose a person receives the gift of teaching, and he exercises his gift through the ministry of preaching. And suppose another person exercises his gift through the ministry of writing. A third person may exercise his gift of teaching through a ministry of counseling. In each case, the same gift expresses itself through various ministries — preaching, writing, counseling."[6]

In the example used by Kinghorn, the Holy Spirit gives the gift of teaching, the Son places the teacher in one of three areas of ministry, and the Father uses that form of ministry to bring about His desired results. Too often, we are not only guilty of trying to control the gift or the ministry, but also the results. Isaiah 55:11 points out that God's word "shall not return unto me void: but it shall accomplish that which I please, and it shall prosper in the thing whereto I sent it." If we allow Him to give us the gift, the ministry and the opportunity, He will bring the results He desires from His proclaimed word. I Corinthians 3:7 says it is "God that giveth the increase."

It must be understood here that the chart is only one example of how God gives and uses the spiritual gifts. Each gift could be categorized in a similar manner, the list going on endlessly. The most important thing we must remember is that the Lord has given us whatever spiritual gift He saw fit and we must allow Him to lead us into whatever ministry He sees fit and to bring whatever desire He sees fit. It all boils down to surrender and availability. As we surrender our lives and make ourselves available, we will then free the Lord to move each of us into exciting and fulfilling ministries.

Now What?

Anyone familiar with Scripture knows there are spiritual gifts. I want to reaffirm that God has given to everybody in His family at least one spiritual gift and everybody in His family has a responsibility to use their gifts. It is important that the common misconceptions mentioned in this chapter be cleared up so that a *proper biblical foundation* is established so that everybody knows where the spiritual gifts come from. In other words, all of God's children need to know they are gifted and why they are gifted.

FOOTNOTES

1   McRae, William, *The Dynamics of Spiritual Gifts* (The Zondervan Corporation: Grand Rapids, 1976) Pages 35-36.
2   Clinton, Bobby, *Spiritual Gifts* (West Indies Mission: Coral Gables, 1975) Page 7.
3   Ryrie, Charles, *The Holy Spirit* (Moody Press, Chicago: 1965) Page 83.
4   Ibid, Page 84.
5   *Liberty Commentary On The New Testament* (Liberty Press, Lynchburg: 1978) Page 414.
6   Kinghorn, Kenneth Cain, *Gifts of the Spirit* (Abingdon Press, Nashville: 1976) Pages 36-37.

CHAPTER TWO

REVIEW QUESTIONS:

1. Which Christians have spiritual gifts, and when did they receive them?

2. Compare the "gifts of the Spirit" and the "fruit of the Spirit".

3. What part does each member of the Trinity play in spiritual gifts?

DISCUSSION QUESTIONS:

1. What are some of the areas that you thought were spiritual gifts before studying this chapter which are not listed in the Scriptures? How does a proper perspective in these areas affect your thinking about the ministry of the church?

2. Why is it important for churches to recognize the spiritual gifts of women and to help them develop those gifts?

3. What part does humility play in the development and use?

CHAPTER THREE

SPIRITUAL GIFTS AND THEIR RELATIONSHIP
TO THE BELIEVER

At a recent Sunday School convention I taught two workshops, one titled "Teaching Spiritual Gifts in the Sunday School" and the other "How to Discover Your Spiritual Gift". The first workshop attracted 30 people to a room that would seat 35. The second workshop attracted approximately 150 people to the same room. People were standing around the wall behind me as I spoke, double doors on two sides of the room were open with people standing outside in the halls. Approximately 100 people stood willingly during the hour long lecture. Why? They wanted to discover their spiritual gifts. Much contemporary material written on spiritual gifts does an adequate job in helping people to recognize, discover and define what their spiritual gift is. Also, many do a fine job of teaching on the individual parts of the body, but never complete their teaching by assembling the body. The problem is not that Christians do not know what *their* spiritual gifts are. The problem is that most Christians do not know what *a* spiritual gift is. They do not understand the *relationships* of spiritual gifts. They don't understand how a spiritual gift relates to their lives, other people's lives, the local church or to the body of Christ as a whole. To give John J. Christian a new name and make him John J. Exhorter Christian is only doing him an injustice. Having a new name or title does not make him any better Christian or give him any more understanding of himself or of others around him.

Under close observation, nine identifying marks of a spiritual gift are revealed. An understanding of those characteristics will help the believer to understand better how the spiritual gift he already has will help him serve the Lord more effectively.

A Spiritual Gift Is The Primary Channel By Which The Holy Spirit Can Minister *Through* The Believer

In the courtyard of a quaint little church in a French village there stood a beautiful marble statue of Jesus with his hands outstretched. One day during World War II a bomb struck near the statue and mutilated it. After the battle was over and the enemy had passed through, the citizens of the village decided to find the pieces of their beloved statue and reconstruct it. Though the statue was no work of art by Michelangelo or Bernini, it was a part of their lives and they loved it. Patiently they gathered the broken pieces and reassembled it. Even the scars on the body added to its beauty. But there was one problem. They were unable to find the hands of the statue. "A Christ without hands is not Christ at all," someone expressed in sorrow. "Hands with scars, yes. But what's a Lord without hands? We need a new statue."

Then someone else came along with another idea, and it prevailed. A brass plaque was attached at the base of the statue which read, "I have no hands but your hands."

Some years later someone saw that inscription and wrote the following lines:

> I have no hands but your hands to do my work today.
> I have no feet but your feet to lead men on the way.
> I have no tongue but your tongue to tell men how I died.
> I have no help but your help to bring men to God's side.

A spiritual gift is the primary channel by which the Holy Spirit can minister through the believer. Without spiritual gifts men can minister one to another only in the flesh. Spiritual gifts are God's provision for the Holy Spirit to minister to man, through man (I Corinthians 12:25).

Stop and consider the importance of this definition, for only through spiritual gifts can men minister to one another with the *full* power of the Holy Spirit.

Years ago, in a small farming town, there was a grain mill beside a stream which flowed out of the hills. The most evident part of the building was the wheel which caught the water from the stream. Inside the building, an axle ran from the wheel to the grinding stone assembly that ground the grain which was delivered by the farmers. The grain was ground into flour for the townspeople to buy or the farmer to have for his own use. The source of power for the grindstone came from the water in the stream which flowed into the paddles of the wheel and turned it, thereby turning the grindstone.

One morning, the miller came to work after a bad storm which had caused several trees in the area to fall and lots of debris to be thrown all over town. When the miller checked around his building before opening the mill, he found there was only a trickle of water flowing down the stream. Limbs and other debris from the storm had dammed the stream, stopping the flow of water. There certainly was not enough power from the water to turn the huge wheel. Something had to be done.

The miller went inside and tried to turn the grinding stone himself. But no matter how much strength he exerted, he could not get the job done. He tried everything he could to provide the necessary power to get the work done which started piling up on him. Finally, he did the most obvious thing and walked upstream about 300 yards and cleared away all the debris and limbs which clogged the stream. Soon he was accomplishing a normal work load and the farmers were loading the flour and meal as fast as he could turn it out.

This is a good picture of Christians trying to carry out the work of the ministry with their own human power. They can carry out some of the work and God blesses every effort to honor Him and do His work on earth. But to attempt effective endeavors for God without the power of the Holy Spirit and the spiritual gifts, is like the miller trying to turn the grindstone without the power of the stream utilizing the wheel to accomplish the task. The water was the power for the mill just as the Holy Spirit is the power at the disposal of the Christian serving God. The wheel was the tool for doing the task just as spiritual gifts are the tools for carrying out the task of reaching and teaching men for Christ. The spiritual gifts are our tools to carry out the work of God. For the miller to grind the grain himself without using the wheel and the power of the stream would be like the Christian doing the work of God without the Holy Spirit's power and the spiritual gifts. For the most effective effort, we need both the full power and the proper tools.

One of the big problems in the church today is that we believe the church to be supernatural in its origin, but not in its operation. When we experience a loss of power and effectiveness, it drives us to rely on human resources in an effort to correct the problem.

Lewis Sperry Chafer writes, "The gift which is wrought by the Spirit is an expression of the Spirit's own ability rather than the mere use of human qualities in the one through whom He works."[1] Spiritual gifts are God's provision for the Holy Spirit to minister THROUGH the believer.

With the GIFTS the Holy Spirit ministers to you through another believer. The believer is not the means but only the instrument the Holy Spirit uses.

Are we getting the job done without spiritual gifts? If we are, it's without the full power of the Holy Spirit. It's the same as having an unsaved man do the job for us.

Remember, God has chosen man to do His work for Him here on earth. Dr. Elmer Towns teaches a principle he calls "The division of labor", based on I Corinthians 3:9, "For we are laborers together with God." His principle simply states, "God will not do what He has commanded you to do, and you cannot do what God has reserved as His authority or duty." Certain areas of ministering to man is reserved by God to be done by men, and God will not step into these prescribed boundaries to do your job for you. For instance, in Luke 6:38, Luke pens, "Give (meaning, you give to God's work) and it shall be given unto you: good measure, pressed down, and shaken together, and running over, shall men give unto your bosom." God's method for giving man material rewards here on earth is *through men*.

So in reality, spiritual gifts involve *God's Stewardship*. He assigns us certain tasks and then equips us to do them in a manner that brings both glory to Him and fulfillment to us (I Peter 4:10, 11). Remember, "The only hands God has are *our* hands."

A Spiritual Gift Is A Supernatural Capacity

A spiritual gift is also a *supernatural capacity* for service to God. Many authors use definitions like, "A supernatural ability," "A God-given ability," "A Spirit-given ability." All these definitions revolve around the word "ability". The word "ability" has been found to be confusing to many older (referring to spiritual not physical age) Christians. Their reasoning being, "I've been a Christian for years and I don't have any 'ability' to do anything in the church; therefore, God must not have given me a gift." In reality, God has given every born-again believer at least one spiritual gift.

A spiritual gift is really not an "ability", but rather a "capacity" to develop an ability. Ability implies that you are able to do something. A proper distinction between the two words is hard to make because descriptive words of both have somewhat the same meanings. The real difference being: an *ability* is a state of being, or present tense, and a *capacity* enables for the future, or future tense. The whole point is that if someone is saved on Monday night and at the moment of his salvation God gives him the gift of teaching, he would not wake up Tuesday morning, a supernatural teacher. But rather, he would wake up with the supernatural capacity (though unknown to him at this point) to develop the supernatural ability of teaching.

We must also distinguish between the gift of the Holy Spirit and the spiritual gifts. The gift of the Holy Spirit is given to the believer at conversion and manifests itself in the presence of the indwelling Spirit who constantly lives personally within the believer, empowering him for service. The spiritual gifts are also given at conversion but manifest themselves as the tools of the Holy Spirit for carrying out the ministry of Christ through the individual believer, requiring the power of the indwelling Holy Spirit in order to be fully effective.

So then, a spiritual gift is a supernatural capacity, freely and graciously given by the sovereign God at the time of your salvation, enabling you to develop the supernatural ability, allowing the Holy Spirit to minister to your fellow man for the purpose of accomplishing His work through you.

A Spiritual Gift Is A Supernatural Desire

In I Timothy 3:1, Paul writes to Timothy saying, "This is a true saying, if a man desire the office of a bishop, he desireth a good work." In verse 2 he goes on to list the qualifications for a bishop. But the question is, what is the very first qualification or requirement for a bishop? You're right, DESIRE. Paul is not directly addressing spiritual gifts here, but the point is, before you can ever become an effective bishop, pastor or anything you must first have the desire.

Many hours of observation have disclosed that when God gives you a spiritual gift, He also gives you a supernatural desire to perform the duties of that gift. For example, if He gives you the gift of showing mercy, He will give you a supernatural desire to comfort others. If evangelism, He will give a supernatural desire to see many lost people won to Christ. As the believer grows and matures, the desire will grow stronger.

Channeled desire equals success. Desire has been determined to be the number one factor behind *all* accomplishment. When studying the lives of great and successful people you will find desire for accomplishment was the underlying ingredient for their success. But ordinary desire will not build much more than mediocrity. The supernatural desire given you with your spiritual gift starts small and undeveloped; it alone will never build a champion for Christ. It takes what the secular "success teachers" call *a burning desire*, or what the Bible calls a *burden*. Only a *burden* can do the extraordinary or build a champion for Christ.

So you don't misunderstand, the word *burden* has both a negative and positive connotation. I am speaking of the positive meaning "A motivating force from within that makes a demand on one's resources, whether material (I Thessalonians 2:6) or spiritual (Galatians 6:2, Revelation 2:24) or religious (Acts 15:28) or emotional."² A *burden* is an unsatisfiable hunger gnawing at your soul. It is a burning in your heart to do what God has called you to do. It is what drives you that second mile.

If it takes a *burden* to make a champion, then how does one get a burden? You must start with the desire given you with your spiritual gift and feed it and challenge it with reading, teaching and preaching of the Word. This will start your desire growing toward a burden. In other words, a *burden* will surface only after one is either convicted by the Holy Spirit through the preaching of the Word, or when one goes through practical training in the area that appeals to his desire. Otherwise, a desire will die on the vine and never grow into a *burden*. When it comes to spiritual gifts you could say, "Use it or lose it."

Spiritual Gifts Are The Tools For Doing The Work Of The Ministry.

Spiritual gifts are the tools for building the church. Ephesians 4:12 says gifts are given, "For the perfecting of the saints, for the work of the ministry, for the edifying of the body of Christ."

Meet "Puzzled Pete". Pete, like many Christians, has the tool given him, but he doesn't know what it's to be used for — "Should I dig a hole with it, or saw a board, or maybe I should mix cement with it?" How can we do the work of the ministry properly if we don't recognize which tools we have and why they are used. This would be like taking a man out of the jungle, giving him a box of tools and sending him out to build a house. If no one showed him the purpose of each tool and how to use it, it is very doubtful he would ever get the job done. However, if he was committed and determined to overcome his frustrations, mistakes and failures, he might get a house built; although, I think many of us would not want to buy it.

One thing of which we can all be certain, we need to learn how to recognize and use the tools God has given each of us. It will make us more effective. You see, God will never give us a hammer and ask us to saw a board, nor will He give us a saw and ask us to drive nails. On the contrary, if God wants us to cut boards, He will give us a saw and if He wants us to drive nails He will give us a hammer.

A Spiritual Gift Is The Source Of Joy In Your Christian Life.

When someone gives you an earthly gift, such as for your birthday or at Christmas, you receive the gift with joy. However, the greatest joy comes when you are able to use that gift in some part of your life. For example, when a lady receives gloves from a friend, she receives a great amount of joy when wearing them with a special outfit and remembering the person's friendship. So it is with the spiritual gifts. We receive them with joy, but the greatest joy comes with using them in the ministry for the glory of God.

There is no other way you can be as fulfilled as when you are using the spiritual gifts God has given you.

Several Greek words are used in the New Testament that are translated "gift" or "spiritual gift". Let's examine them:

(1.) *Doma*: Luke 11:13, Ephesians 4:8. The word means "a present, to build, a gift."[3]

(2.) (a.) *Charisma*: Romans 12:6, I Corinthians 12:4, 9, 28, 30, 31. If I were to ask you if you were Charismatic, many of you would say, "No." But, the truth is, all Christians are Charismatic. The Charismatic Movement just took its name from charisma because of the movement's emphasis on the miraculous gifts. The word means, "A (divine) gratuity, a (spiritual) endowment, a religious qualification, a (free) gift."[4] The word *Charisma* is a form of the word *Charis*.

(b.) *Charis*: Most places in the New Testament this word is interpreted "grace", meaning unmerited favor. The root word of both of these words is the word *Char*.

(c.) *Char.* meaning joy, happiness or fulfillment. The basic idea taught through this original word usage is summed up by the authors of the *Liberty Commentary*, "As you use the gift which God gave you by His grace, it produces the greatest amount of joy or fulfillment, spiritually, in your life." It goes on to say, "There is a definite interrelationship in the root idea of these words."[5]

Your spiritual gift is the source of joy in your Christian life. When you are using the gift given you, you will be able to function with maximum fulfillment and minimum frustration. Using your gift for the service of Christ is the only way you can fulfill that God-given inner need to serve your fellow man.

Every Christian should have a "personal ministry". Your personal ministry should reflect your spiritual gift or at least allow itself to be manifest. What is a "personal ministry"? — That which you do for God that benefits someone else.

A Spiritual Gift Is A Divine Motivator

This concept, made popular by Bill Gothard, is possibly the greatest single contribution to the area of spiritual gifts. It recognizes that spiritual gifts are not just a title God gives to the believer, but a major motivating factor in the lives of the recipients.

Many books on the subject of motivation will summarize by saying something like this, "The best possible way to motivate people to a task is to find people who are already motivated." If you are planning to use external means of motivation, you might find such a statement discouraging, especially if no one around you is motivated. But the good news is, every Christian *is* motivated, in the sense that every Christian has a spiritual gift. Along with that spiritual gift comes a divine, supernatural, internal motivation from God to perform the responsibilities of the gift.

The Christian with *gift awareness* finds himself saying, "That person has a need. I can fill that need with my gift." Or, he may know another believer with a gift that fulfills that need and he directs the two people to one another. The words may not be exact, but the attitude is there. That capacity and supernatural desire mentioned earlier becomes the motivator and causes actions to take place without the necessity of outside motivation and prompting. In fact the Holy Spirit is actually doing the motivating from within.

A Spiritual Gift Divinely Influences One's Motives.

Suppose you had just bought a new Cadillac Seville. You had dreamed all your life about having such a car. You saved, invested and sacrificed so that you could finally buy the dream car you always wanted. As you drive home from the dealership in your pride and joy, you pass a little boy on the side of the road. He is poised with a rock in his hand as if to throw it toward your new car. You cringe as you view him sideways, for you see a nightmare coming true. The little boy fires the dreaded missile into the passenger side door of your new Cadillac. You hear it hit, slam on the brakes, skid to a stop, jump out of the car, feeling the anger overtaking your entire being. As you head for the little scrounge, you ask yourself what the penalty is for murdering an eleven-year-old who just shattered your dream. Before you can say anything to him, the little boy cries and says, "Mister, I'm sorry I dented your car, but my little brother fell and broke his leg and that's the only way I could get a car to stop." Suddenly, your motives are changed from anger to understanding and a willingness to help. Such is the case with our motives for serving God and helping others. We can understand why people behave or think the way they do when we understand their spiritual gifts. As we learn the characteristics, strengths and weaknesses of each gift, it helps us to see our brethren, and even our families in a different light.

One lady, after studying gifts, remarked, "Now I know why Harry is always down the street doing for someone else what I tried to get him to do at home." He had the gift of service. By understanding his motives she found it easier to accept him.

There would be fewer church squabbles if more Christians understood what motivates those who have gifts differing from their own.

A Spiritual Gift Is A Divine Calling And Divine Responsibility

Remember when you were a kid and enjoyed singing, *I'm in the Lord's Army*? To adults it has been preached, "You're in the Lord's Army," and during the invitation comes the question, "Will you volunteer for the Lord's Army?" A stirring invitation? Yes! A way to get commitments? Yes! Good theology? No! The Lord's Army *is not* a volunteer army. The question is *not*, "Will you volunteer for the Lord's

Army?" The question is, "Are you a draft dodger or not?" If you are a Christian, you *are* in His Army whether you want to be or not (Acts 1:8, Ephesians 2:10). God has equipped you for battle (your spiritual gift), and you have a divine responsibility to use that gift.

In observation of Ephesians 4:1, you will note it is Paul's introduction to the subject of spiritual gifts. He said, "I therefore, the prisoner of the Lord, beseech you that ye walk worthy of the vocation wherewith ye are called." In verse 11, he lists the principles concerning spiritual gifts. The important thing to notice is that when Paul starts talking about spiritual gifts he begins by talking about your calling or vocation. I have seen several lists where an asterisk (*) is put by several gifts and at the bottom of the page the author would write something like, "This gift may require a calling from God." The truth is, they *all* require a calling from God and with each one comes an automatic calling. *What God has gifted you to do, He has called you to do, and what He has called you to do, He has gifted you to do.* When He gives you the gift, He gives you the responsibility to use it. It is not whether to make this service your occupation. Every believer has been called into full-time service; however, not every Christian has been called to make that service his occupation or means of supporting his family.

Another passage speaking of the responsibility that comes with your spiritual gift is I Peter 4:10, "As every man hath received the gift, even so minister the same one to another, as good stewards of the manifold (varied) grace of God." This passage speaks of spiritual gifts in a more general sense than the other passages. Nevertheless, Peter *is* speaking of spiritual gifts in the light of stewardship. A steward is one who is entrusted with and held accountable for something that belongs to his master.

In Matthew 25:14-30, we study the parable of the talents. So as not to confuse you, the talents mentioned here are not natural talents, spiritual gifts or any type of an ability. This talent was a very large denomination of money.

We can gain a Biblical principle of accountability from this passage. "For the kingdom of Heaven is as a man travelling into a far country, who called his own servants, and delivered unto them his goods. And unto one he gave five talents, to another two, and to another one: to every man according to his several (capacity) ability" (Matthew 25:14-15). The word several, today, is best interpreted *capacity*; therefore, the verse is saying, "according to the capacity of his ability." For example, you may have the gift of pastor-teacher with the capacity to shepherd 5000 people. Therefore, God will allow you to exercise your gift according to that capacity and hold you accountable for it at that level. Another may have the same gift but only have the capacity to shepherd 20 people. In God's eyes, the latter is no less. This is what God will hold him accountable for. You are accountable for the capacity as well as the gift. Think of your gift as a bucket and contents of the bucket as its capacity. God may give some men a ten gallon bucket while He gives others a two gallon bucket.

The parable goes on to say that when the master returned home, the servant to whom he had given five talents had doubled them and gave his master back ten, and the servant who had two also doubled his, to which the master replied, "Well done thou good and faithful servant, thou hast been faithful over a few things, I will make thee ruler over many things" (Matthew 25:21). But the servant who had the one talent had taken it and buried it. He was a poor servant. He had not properly used that which his master had entrusted to him.

This might be a good question for you to consider at this point: at the Judgment, when you have the opportunity to stand before Christ, what will He say to you? Will He say, "Well done thou good and faithful servant," or might He say, as He did to the third servant in verse 26, "Thou wicked and slothful (lazy) servant." The Bible plainly states, "For we must *all* appear before the judgment seat of Christ, that every man may receive the things done in his body according to that he hath done, whether it be good or bad" (II Corinthians 5:10).

Spiritual Gifts Are The Building Blocks Of The Church.

In his book on witnessing, David Innes talks about his first church. He admits being too program centered, even though people came to Christ and the church grew. He says, "I started with the programs and not the people. Eventually, I began to dry up. Instead of starting with the people's needs and designing programs, ministry, teaching, etc., to fit into and meet their needs, I always started with the programs and tried to get people to fit into those programs. For some, the programs happened to meet their needs. But for many they didn't and these people were left out.

"I even quoted Bible verses to support my programs and get people to do what I wanted them to do. If I were there today as pastor, I would start with the people first, find out exactly what their needs were and design all programs, teaching and preaching to meet their needs and not mine, being people centered rather than being program centered. *The New Testament is all but silent on methodology and is remarkably free of programs,*" he observed.[6]

A church should be built with people instead of programs. Many churches will build super organizations and super programs and try to fit their people into them. What we need to do is start with the people and their gifts, with their burdens, motivations and abilities and build the church with them.

It has been said, "Never use a great people to build a great church, but use a great church to build a great people." On the contrary we *should* use a great people to build a great church and then use a great church to meet the needs of a great people. It is an unending cycle — people ministering to people through the living organism called the church.

The world even agrees with the philosophy of building on people. Management teachers and writers today are also emphasizing this philosophy, saying "The key to make this type of man effective is to start with the person, find out what his strengths are, and put him in a position where he can make full use of his strengths. Never start with the job and make the man fit into the job or the program. Start with the man and make the job or the program fit into his strengths. This will automatically minimize and render harmless his weaknesses. This is being people centered in leadership."[7] Business is the same as the church — you need to build with the means not the task.

But someone will ask about Jesus saying, "*I* will build my church" (Matthew 16:18). Yes, He did say that, and I Corinthians 3:9 says, "For we are laborers together with God." Christ *will* build His church, but He's going to do it through you. Chuck Millhuff says it nicely, "God can if I will."

Now What?

A spiritual gift is not just a superficial name we add to a believer once he is saved. A spiritual gift is something that has a hold on the believer's life and manifests itself through his life. The spiritual gifts remove the frustration and confusion from serving God. When one learns the definition of what a gift is, he realizes that it is not just another characteristic of the spirit filled life, but it is the way the spirit filled life manifests itself. What the spirit filled life is all about is for the believer to take the area where God has equipped him and put it into service for Him.

Regardless of what gift is present in a believer's life, it has certain effects on his life. The gift strongly influences the desires and motives of living and ministry. There are strengths in each gift which can influence the motives both for good and for the bad. It is such a strong part of the motives, that it can be truthfully said that if one is miserable in the service where he is now, chances are he is not exercising his spiritual gift.

People are motivated to action for two reasons: either they *have to* or they *want to*. Spiritual gifts are the "want to" of Christian service.

FOOTNOTES

1   Chafer, Lewis Sperry, *Systematic Theology, Pneumotology* (Dallas Seminary Press: Dallas, 1974) Page 216.
2   Vines, W. E., *Vine's Expository Dictionary of New Testament Words* (MacDonald Publishing Company: McLean,) Page 159.
3   Strong, James, *Strong's Exhaustive Concordance of the Bible*, Page 24.
4   Ibid, Page 77.
5   Falwell, Jerry et al, *Liberty Commentary On the New Testament* (Liberty Press: Lynchburg, 1978) Page 77.
6   Innes, David, *I Hate Witnessing* (Visions House Publishers: Ventura, 1983) Page 107.
7   Drucker, Peter, *The Effective Executive* (Harper & Row Publishers: New York, 1966) Page 75.

CHAPTER THREE

REVIEW QUESTIONS:

1. How does a "capacity" differ from a talent or ability?

2. Who belongs in the "Lord's Army"? How has God equipped His army?

3. If God has given you a gift, what else has He done?

DISCUSSION QUESTIONS:

1. What has God given you an unusually strong desire to do in His work? Which spiritual gift does that correspond with? If you had that spiritual gift, how would you develop it?

2. Discuss a situation that has arisen in your life that changed your motives?

3. How important are motives to actions? Can you determine another person's motives by their actions?

CHAPTER FOUR

SPIRITUAL GIFTS AND THEIR RELATIONSHIP
TO THE WILL OF GOD

Whenever a handful of Christians get together, it is just a matter of time till someone brings up the subject of *the will of God.* It's a subject with which we are all much concerned. We want to know who to marry, where to live, where to go to church; even simpler questions like what kind of car does He want me to buy, or what kind of home? How many children should we have? Mostly, we want answers to questions where the Bible is not clear. There are no verses to say, "thou shalt have six children" or "thou shalt have two children." Yet these are all subjects that greatly concern us.

We are rightfully concerned about wrong turns. For instance, it has been said that in the United States alone there are more than 23,000 ways to make a living. According to some surveys, approximately eighty-eight percent of the American work force are working in jobs they do not like or they would not choose for a career. The Christian should not be included in those statistics, for he has a God who can lead him in the paths best suited to him. If that is true, how does one find God's will or direction for his life?

It is interesting to see that two of the major passages where Paul writes about spiritual gifts begin by talking about the will of God. In Romans 12:2, Paul speaks of that "good, acceptable, and perfect will of God." This is his introduction to spiritual gifts. So, if we want to know what is that good, acceptable, and perfect will of God for our lives, then it must have something to do with spiritual gifts.

However, to address only the will of God and the relationship of spiritual gifts to God's will would be a mistake. It is necessary to address a complete overview of God's will in order to understand how spiritual gifts relate to it.

There are many good books written on this subject of God's will, but there are just as many that may have unintentionally misled you. So let's start off by addressing what you may have found confusing.

The Will Of God For Your Life Is Not Bad.

Many Christians fear the will of God. Ray Stedman in his book, *Body Life*, says, "Somewhere the idea has found deep entrenchment in Christian circles that doing what God wants you to do is always unpleasant; Christians must always make choices between doing what they want to do and being happy, and doing what God wants them to do and being completely miserable."[1] Nothing could be further from the truth. Many Christians think that if they give in to the will of God, God will strip them naked, take everything they own, give them a loincloth and send them to Africa. After all isn't that God's calling to everybody — to be a missionary?

Have you ever heard it said, "Don't say that, or that's just what God will make you do," as if God was looking for ways to torture you? God is our loving Father and He wants only the best for His children. He is not going to put us in any situation that will compromise our effectiveness to serve Him.

How contrary that would be to God's nature. Why can we justify looking at God's will for His children being bad while His will for the unbeliever is to provide deliverance from sin, oppression and judgment? Galatians 1:4 says, "Who gave Himself for our sins, that He might deliver us from this present evil world, according to the will of God and our Father." God is not willing to deliver us from "this present evil world" in order to place us back into misery. Part of the deliverance we receive through Christ is deliverance from those things which make us miserable.

One pastor, after studying spiritual gifts and the will of God, said, "A great surprise in my life was to discover God's will would make me happy."

God's Will For Your Life Is *Not* Fixed.

"One of the most amazing and practical truths of the Bible is that God has a definite plan for your life." "God has a blueprint for your life." "God's will is like a road map with your trip laid out for you." These are statements taken from various introductions of materials written on God's will. "A definite plan", "a blueprint", "a planned trip"; such terminology can confuse and discourage you. "I am thirty-eight (or whatever number) years old and just finding out that God has a definite plan for my life. Surely, I have blown it many times by now. My blueprint does not even resemble the original structure that God has planned, so why even bother with it now? I am bound to arrive at a different destination than God has planned," speaks the voice of discouragement.

Many Christians have married unsaved mates only to find years later it was not God's will for them. Now, some want to "trade in" their mate, which is not God's will either. The point is, we have all made many mistakes along the way and the idea that God's will is non-bendable, fixed or non-variable can put undue pressure on us.

And it's GOOD NEWS that God has many provisions in His will for our failures and shortcomings. You haven't missed the boat. He has even allowed you the privilege of making some decisions and choices while remaining in His will.

It is plain from a study of the Scriptures which speak of the will of God that the specific will of God deals with spiritual qualities and the spiritual condition of believers rather than a deed or specific place of service or task.

God's Will For Your Life Is Not Lost.

Many books and messages include remarks like, "How to find the will of God," "Seeking God's will," or "Searching for God's will" as if it were lost. They leave us wandering aimlessly through life until we can stumble upon God's will. There is nothing to find or discover. I am not condemning the use of the terms. It is common to use them; however, we do need to recognize that we can confuse ourselves with them.

I use the term "discover" in presenting this material on gifts (Discover your Spiritual Gift!) only because it is a term to which everyone relates. A better term to use would be "recognize".

Psalms 40:8 says, "I delight to do thy will, O my God: yea, thy law is within my heart." If you notice the word "is" is italicized. This means the translator added it to help us better understand the passage. Read it without the "is". Right! Now we see "thy will" and "thy law" are one and the same. They are both within our hearts. In fact, it could say, "Thy will is Thy law within my heart."

God's will for your life is part of your very being as a believer. We do not have to discover it or find it at all. What we need to do is learn to *recognize* what is already there.

God's Will Is Not Revealed To Others.

Isn't it funny that when this subject is brought up, how much other people know of God's will for *your* life? They have advice as to just what God wants you to do, yet in many cases they are very confused as to what God's will is for their own lives. God will reveal His will for your life to *you*, not to someone else.

Several years ago, my wife and I were "searching" for God's will for our lives. We visited a mission camp in Pennsylvania. We spent a lot of time with their counselors. We were very confused since at that time we had no idea what God's will was for our lives. But also, there was no doubt *they knew* what God's will for our lives was. They were certain God had called us to missions and we were resisting God's will by not accepting the call. At that point we made a decision to go elsewhere to a school and pursue a course of study which which had nothing to do with missions. Our present plans still have nothing to do with missions. We have not doubted for one minute we made the right decision. My wife and I are totally convinced that we are in God's will. Yet, when we left that camp, the people there were saying that we were refusing to accept or do God's will.

I am not speaking of legitimate counseling when someone points out to you, with the use of the Word of God, principles that will help you determine the will of God or direct statements from the Bible that are clearly the will of God. (Hopefully this chapter is doing this.) Nor do I want to give young people the incentive to ignore their parents. But, I am talking about people who are trying to impose God's will for their lives on you. The principle to learn is, *God will reveal His will for your life to you.* You will have to make the final decision.

In the case of a married couple, He is going to reveal it to both. He will never divide a couple.

God's Will Is Not Based On Circumstances.

In Judges 6:37-40 we have the story of Gideon and the fleece. From this story we have gleaned a popular phrase in discerning God's will — "putting out the fleece".

Today when we "put out the fleece", we are setting up circumstances and asking God to fit them. We are saying, "If you want me to do that, God, then You must do this."

Decisions based on circumstances in your life are based on having a super amount of faith. Some Christians can make life-altering decisions based on circumstances, but the point to make is that *most Christians cannot.* Most Christians have not developed the faith it takes to make these decisions.

Too many Christians would be like the elderly Scottish lady who went to country homes to sell thread, buttons and shoe strings. When she came to an unmarked crossroad, she would throw a stick into the air to determine which road she'd take that day. Observed throwing the stick into the air several times one day, she was asked why. She replied, "It has pointed every time to the road going to the right, and I want to go on the road to the left, it looks smoother." She kept throwing the stick until it pointed the direction she wanted to go. This principle of "putting out the fleece" and using circumstances should not be used this way, of course. We usually use circumstances only for major decisions. We trust in our own intelligence to make little decisions. But when a big decision comes up, we will "put out the fleece" and in most cases it will not work. I realize in some cases it may work, so I want to be careful not to entirely discard this principle. I will say more about it when we get to the section on faith.

The Will Of God Is Not Contrary To The Word Of God.

You would never have to pray this prayer, "Lord, You know I am out of work and have been out for a long time. The bills are piling up. We don't have money to buy groceries. The children don't have shoes. Father, is it Your will that I rob the service station on the corner so we will have money to take care of our financial needs?" Now, of course, this is a foolish prayer because it is contrary to the Word of God which says, "Thou shalt not steal" (Exodus 20:15). That might be an extreme example because it is so obvious you would not pray about being a thief. But there are often principles in the Bible which we should use in determining the will of God.

The main principle is: *anything that is contrary to the Word of God is also contrary to the will of God.*

If we can't look to these things to help us recognize the will of God for our lives, then where can we look? In the Word of God. So let's look to see what God's will is for your life.

THE WILL OF GOD IS:[2]

God's Will For Your Life Is That You Be SAVED.

Look at II Peter 3:9. "The Lord is not slack concerning his promise, as some men count slackness; but is longsuffering to us-ward, not willing that any should perish, but that all should come to repentance." Therefore, God's will for your life is for you to be saved. God is not willing that any man should die and go to Hell. Romans 8:7 and 8 says, "Because the carnal mind is enmity against God; for it is not subject to the law of God, neither indeed can be. So then they that are in the flesh cannot please God." This might be a simple statement to make, but if a person is not saved, he is not in the will of God.

God's Will For Your Life Is That You Be SANCTIFIED

I Thessalonians 4:3 and 4 says, "For this is the will of God, even your sanctification, that ye should abstain from fornication: That every one of you should know how to possess his vessel in sanctification and honor." Sanctification means to make holy, pure, set apart. As you read forward in this passage, you'll see God intends for you to be holy or set apart. You are to abstain from fornication. That is purity. You are to be controlled by the Spirit not the flesh and you are not to defraud your brother. God's will for your life is that you are to be sanctified.

God's Will For Your Life Is That You Be SPIRIT FILLED.

Ephesians 5:17 and 18 says, "Wherefore be ye not unwise, but understanding what the will of the Lord is. And be not drunk with wine, wherein is excess; but be filled with the Spirit." To be filled with the Spirit means to be controlled by the Spirit. Verse 18 is an excellent verse to exemplify this. Paul uses it to show us what being controlled by the Spirit is. He says, "And be not drunk with wine." Have you ever seen anyone drunk, full of wine, walking down the street? He has a hard time walking because the wine that fills him has total control of his body. The same is true with the Holy Spirit. When you are filled with the Spirit, then the Spirit will have control of you.

God's Will For Your Life Is That You Are SUBMISSIVE.

I Peter 2:13-15 says, "Submit yourselves to every ordinance of man for the Lord's sake: whether it be to the king, as supreme; Or unto governors, as unto them that are sent by him for the punishment of evildoers, and for the praise of them that do well. For so is the will of God, that with well doing ye may put to silence the ignorance of foolish men:" This passage indicates that we are to be subject to those God has put in authority over us. We are to be subject to God, to our pastor, to our civil leaders, to the policemen. Why should we be subject to these people? (In many cases we are talking about being subject to non-Christians.) The scripture says that we "put to silence the ignorance of foolish (unsaved) men." We should not have a rebellious spirit. A rebellious spirit is one of the first things someone will spot in you. One pastor states, "We are training leaders at our school and you will never become a good leader until you can become a good follower."

You might say, "That doesn't pertain to me, because God hasn't called me to be a leader." But on the contrary, God has called us all to be leaders. We need to be outstanding as leaders in the eyes of the non-Christian world. We all have that responsibility to help lead every one of those people to the saving knowledge of Jesus Christ. At one time or another, we all have leadership roles.

One of the biggest areas where Christians do not submit themselves to civil leaders is simply in obeying the speed limit. If we are guilty of speeding, we show our children and others around us that we don't have to submit if we think they are unfair or unjust laws and we have many valid reasons to violate them. But, God's will for our lives is that we be submissive.

God's Will For Your Life Is That You SUFFER.

I Peter 4:19 states, "Wherefore let them that suffer according to the will of God commit the keeping of their souls to him in well doing, as unto a faithful Creator." Let's look at I Peter 3:17, "For it is better, if the will of God be so, that ye suffer for well doing, than for evil doing." Many of you are thinking, "Boy! Do I qualify for this one." But look again at the passage, it says for "well doing". Most of our suffering is not for well doing but for improper or wrong doings. As I look back over my life, I can see times that I suffered both physically and emotionally. But if I am truthful, most of the time it was for "evil doing" or ignorance, or violation of scriptural principles that God has laid down for me. By violating them, I in turn suffered.

There are many levels in this area of suffering. We think of Christians having to suffer in Communist countries where they cannot gather to worship, and where many have been beaten or put to death for their faith in Jesus Christ. This is what we think of as suffering. We can thank God that we are living in a free country where we can share our faith and we do not have to suffer as some of these other Christians. But the truth is, many Christians will suffer if they are willing to live an obedient life. Many Christians will suffer if they are willing to take a stand, or live by the principles that are laid down in the Scriptures.

Many businessmen do suffer because the rules governing business today are no longer based on Judeo-Christian ethics. In a lot of businesses the motto is "get all you can, can all you get," or "do it any way possible." Many Christian businessmen bid on jobs knowing if they don't bend a little rule or if they stay in line scripturally, they have no chance of getting the job. But if they just twist the rules a little bit and do something that is acceptable in the business world, they can get the order. Yet they know in their hearts Christ will condemn them. The Christian businessman who takes a stand will often lose his work to competitors. It makes business harder on him. It makes him suffer.

The question is, "Why should we suffer?" Let's look at I Peter 2:21, "For even hereunto were ye called: because Christ also suffered for us, leaving us an example, that ye should follow his steps." God's will for your life is that you suffer.

God's Will For Your Life Is That You Are SERVING

In Romans 12:1-3 it states, "I beseech you therefore, brethren, by the mercies of God, that ye present your bodies a living sacrifice, holy, acceptable unto God, which is your reasonable service. And be not conformed to this world: but be ye transformed by the renewing of your mind, that ye may prove what is that good, and acceptable, and perfect, will of God. For I say, through the grace given unto me, to every man that is among you, not to think of himself more highly than he ought to think; but to think soberly, according as God hath dealt to every man the measure of faith." The one word that separates Christianity from other religions is SERVING.

In most material addressing the will of God, this is the most commonly used passage. Bible commentaries offer a variety of interpretations of what this passage means. Many commentaries have this passage backwards. To make clear what I am saying, there is an old rule of thumb about working with the book of Romans. It is: if you discover what the "therefore" is "there for" you will understand the passage. The passage of Romans 12:1 starts off "I beseech you *therefore*". Using this rule you have to look backwards to see what Paul was talking about. And in this case, he has been talking about the goodness (mercies) of God. Now he is saying, "Therefore, based on the goodness of God, you need to be in service. You need to make your bodies a living sacrifice (in contrast to the dead sacrifices of the Old Testament) and be in service to God. Now, I am going to tell you how to do it and what you have to do it with." This is his introduction to spiritual gifts. Paul is basically saying, "If you are going to be in that good, acceptable and perfect will of God, you will have to use your spiritual gifts." Paul is now giving you the practical application based on the previous chapters of doctrine. He is saying, "If you are going to serve God in a task oriented way, in a way that you will accomplish something with your life, in a way that you will accomplish something for God, here is the practical way to fulfill the doctrine that I have been teaching you."

In a parallel passage, Ephesians 4, Paul starts off, "I therefore, the prisoner of the Lord, beseech you that ye walk worthy of the vocation wherewith ye are called." Again, it is interesting to see that "the vocation wherewith ye are called" is referring to a calling for your life, God's will for your life. In another passage, I Peter 4:10, Peter states, "As every man hath received the gift, even so *minister the same one to another*, as good stewards of the manifold grace of God." These Scriptures talk about service. Service is making your body a living sacrifice, doing something with your body.

In summary of our first six principles, think of Romans 12 as a capstone passage for the other five principles that we have looked at: saved, sanctified, Spirit filled, submissive, and suffering. It is a kind of summary statement of all of the others, because when you are doing all these other five principles you are making your body a living sacrifice. A living sacrifice for service to Christ, which Paul says is "your reasonable service." God's will for your life is that you are serving.

At this point you may say, "These are six pretty good principles, but you have not answered the question that is tormenting me about God's will. I can understand that these things are revealed in the Word of God as being His will for my life. I understand that part of God's will for my life, but what I need is to find a means of determining the unrevealed things. These principles you covered are all revealed in the Word of God. There are a lot of things that I need to make decisions on that are not in the Word of God."

At this point let me bring out a different principle. *God will never reveal to you His unrevealed will if you are not willing to do His revealed will.* A man might say, "I know that God's will for my life is for me not to smoke, but what I really need to know is should we make this move that is coming up?" "I know God's will for my life is that I don't lose my temper, but what I really need to know is how do I make this other decision in my life?" Well, that leads us right into the seventh principle by asking, "What is God's will for my life?"

God's Will For Your Life Is. . .

I shared with you earlier about the mission camp and how pressure was put on us to make a decision to go into missions. We even got to the point where we did a little bit of arguing and some debating. Real pressure was put on us when one of the counselors finally put me on the spot by asking, "How can you be so positive that God doesn't want you to go into missions?" Without thinking or understanding I blurted out what I would later discover to be a very important principle in determining God's will and decision-making.

I said, "Because I don't want to!" This brings us to the last principle. Very seldom will you hear this principle taught, and undoubtedly it's because it can be so easily misused. I didn't begin teaching the will of God with principle number seven because it could be very misleading.

In understanding the danger of this principle, I want to emphasize very strongly that if you are *saved*, if you are *sanctified*, if you are *Spirit filled*, if you are *submissive*, if you are *suffering* and if you are *serving*, then (and only then) God's will for your life is **whatever you desire**.

That's right, God's will for your life is whatever you desire, whatever you want. If, at this point, you meet all of these qualifications: saved, sanctified, Spirit filled, submissive, suffering and serving, then who do you think is controlling your desires? Who do you think is controlling your wants? It is impossible for a man to practice these six principles and then do things that are undesirable in the sight of God.

The will of God is whatever you desire. Psalms 37:4 says, "Delight thyself also in the Lord; and he shall give thee the desires of thine heart." It is not saying He will give you all the material things you desire. It is saying He will give you the *desires* themselves.

Where should you go to school? Where should you live? What church should you attend? Where should you send your children to school? Wherever you want to. Whatever you want to do. If you are living these principles, then your desire will be God's will for your life because God will put those desires in your heart. He will let you use your innermost feelings to direct your path. "But," comes the argument, "Proverbs 3:6 says, 'He (not we) will direct thy paths.'" Let's be realistic for a minute. God doesn't write on the wall with His finger any more and the U.S. postal service doesn't extend to Heaven, nor can we get direction from super bass-voices from above as in the movies. Without these, all that is left is the Word of God and the Spirit of God. The Spirit indwells us and influences our innermost being. If God wills that you do something contrary to your desire, He will simply change your desire (Philippians 2:13).

I know that the men at the mission camp thought we were being rebellious and not willing to accept God's will for our lives. Now, years later, I can look back and say, "I know that we made the right decision," because God has blessed us and there is no doubt in our minds we are in God's will.

This brings us to an important observation. You and I are not living these six principles perfectly. But, the closer we come to these principles, the closer our decisions will be to pleasing God based on our desires. The more we neglect and stray from these first six principles, the less accurate our "desire" based decisions will be.

Remember *serving* is one of the six principles. The importance of service in relation to decisions based on your desires is made evident in Proverbs 16:3, "Commit thy works unto the Lord, and thy thoughts shall be established."

Test Your Desires.

Another very important observation that must be made at this point is you must be able to distinguish between *desires* and *whims*.

Many advertisers rely on what they call "point of purchase" advertising or, in other words, "whim purchasing". Rarely is an item purchased on a whim a needed item. That is why advertisers use this form of advertising. They know you won't buy it if you think about it. The same is true of decisions made on whims.

Test your desires to see if they are whims. There are basically two tests: *time* and *knowledge*. Whims will seldom stand the test of time. Yet, God-given desires will grow with time. Also weigh your desires against the Word of God. Desires that clash with biblical truths are not put in your heart by God.

The Source Of Desires

So, what is the relationship between God's will and spiritual gifts? First, your gift is always in perfect harmony with the will of God for your life. Remember, *what God has called you to do He has gifted you to do, and what He has gifted you to do, He has called you to do*. Secondly; understanding the will of God for your life is much easier when you know your spiritual gift. The earlier you understand your spiritual gift, the easier it will be to determine the will of God for your life. If your area of service does not correspond with your spiritual gift, you may become discouraged and frustrated and never find out where you really belong. You won't understand yourself, the gifts or other Christians around you. In turn you will eventually become a dropout or end up doing nothing for God. *The key is to teach spiritual gifts in the early stages of the Christian's life.* This will give Christians a better handle on the will of God for their lives and give them more direction as they start their Christian walk.

Now What?

Remember, one of the characteristics of a spiritual gift is "*a supernatural desire*". If God's will for your life is "whatever you desire" and your spiritual gift is a supernatural desire, then your spiritual gift is going to greatly influence what God's will is for your life.

In essence what I am saying is that the will of God is not some superficial mythological truth that we can't really grasp. My observation shows that the will of God is part of the Christian's very being, and that being is strongly influenced by the spiritual gift God has given him.

In light of these facts, it is evident that the emphasis should be shifted from trying to find God's will to walking with God in the Spirit-filled life and to finding and implementing the spiritual gifts. When this is done, the will of God will come naturally.

FOOTNOTES:

[1] Stedman, Ray, *Body Life* (Regal Books, Glendale: 1972) Page 56.

[2] MacArthur, John, *How to Know God's Will* (The Word of Grace Tape Ministry, Sun Valley, CA) Based on several points in MacArthur's outline.

CHAPTER FOUR

REVIEW QUESTIONS:

1. Name the seven things that are God's will for your life.

2. What is the big danger of the teaching of your desires and the will of God?

3. What is the relationship between the will of God and spiritual gifts?

DISCUSSION QUESTIONS:

1. In what areas have you had a problem in the six steps of the spirit-filled life as outlined in this chapter? How can the problem be overcome?

2. Where have you had a problem finding the will of God for your life? What teaching in this chapter about the will of God has helped you see God's will better and how?

3. How could you test your desires?

SECTION TWO

THE GIFTS

INTRODUCTION

In a recent survey we asked the question, "What is your spiritual gift?" Of the 72 adults responding only 15 answered with what could be considered a valid name for a spiritual gift. Twenty-two gave no answer at all. But most amazing of all were the 28 who listed as their gift a term the Bible did not list — many listed fruit of the Spirit. There are 21 gifts listed in the New Testament. However, most Bible scholars will agree on a list of only 18. Because of the closeness of the definitions and characteristics of some gifts, it is felt that the Scriptures use synonyms in some cases. The following lists the gifts and Scripture references and suggests a simplified classification. It also shows which gifts are combined for our study. We will discuss them in detail later.

1. MIRACULOUS GIFTS

Apostle	I Corinthians 12:28; Ephesians 4:11
Tongues	I Corinthians 12:10, 28, 30
Interpretation	I Corinthians 12:10, 30
Miracles	I Corinthians 12:10, 28
Healing	I Corinthians 12:9, 28

2. ENABLING GIFTS

Faith	I Corinthians 12:9
Discernment	I Corinthians 12:10
Wisdom	I Corinthians 12:8
Knowledge	I Corinthians 12:8

3. TEAM GIFTS

Evangelism	Ephesians 4:11
Prophecy	Romans 12:6; Ephesians 4:11, I Corinthians 12:10, 28
Teaching	Romans 12:7; I Corinthians 12:28
Exhortation	Romans 12:8
Pastor/Shepherd	Ephesians 4:11
Showing Mercy	Romans 12:8
Serving	Romans 12:7; I Corinthians 12:28
Giving	Romans 12:8
Administrations	Romans 12:8; I Corinthians 12:28

The Miraculous Gifts

The MIRACULOUS GIFTS are generally known today as *Charismatic Gifts*. The term *Charismatic* has become a generic term and probably takes in a broader base of denominations and groups than would voluntarily add themselves to the terminology. However there are basically five positions (although each has many variations) on the miraculous, or charismatic, gifts.

Number One, the EXTREME CHARISMATIC position contends that gifts are given through a second work of the Holy Spirit and that speaking in tongues is the evidence of the indwelling of the Holy Spirit. This view is rejected by most of Christianity. Those holding this position speak in tongues, although all that speak in tongues do not hold this position. Those in this position usually hold that one must speak in tongues in order to be saved, thus adding to the Scriptures and thereby qualifying as a cult.

Number Two, the CHARISMATIC position contends that all gifts are valid today and are given just as they were in the early church. They say that in order to experience the fullness of the Holy Spirit, all these gifts should be exercised in every local church. They reject the idea that tongues or any gift is *the* evidence of the fulness of the Holy Spirit. Most holding this position would profess having had some kind of charismatic experience at one time or another.

Number Three, the LIMITED-CHARISMATIC position says all gifts are valid today and given just as they were in the early church. However, God distributes these gifts within the "universal church", and different gifts manifest themselves in different local churches. Most of those who hold this position have never had a charismatic experience but are convinced that charismatic doctrine is valid. This is the middle-of-the-road position taken by most publishers and many main line denominations.

Number Four, the NON-CHARISMATIC position says all gifts are *not* valid today; therefore, the miraculous gifts should not be exercised in any church. It is their position that these gifts were given to the early church to establish or validate the authority of those who had the gift, and they were phased out by the end of the first century with the completion of the Canon of Scriptures (the Bible). They do not deny God heals. They deny that God gives any gift that allows man to heal.

Number Five, the ANTI-CHARISMATIC position takes about the same doctrinal stand as the non-charismatic position. But they have a tendency to take the abuses of the Extreme Charismatic and tag all Charismatics with them. Their doctrinal disagreement usually leads to personal attacks. They usually tag all who hold to any of the charismatic positions as false teachers.

The purpose of this material is not to argue the pros and cons of the Charismatic Movement. Nor, is it to establish a doctrine concerning the charismatic gifts.

I wish to avoid the problem with much of the contemporary teaching on spiritual gifts. Many charismatics teach on the miraculous gifts with little or no emphasis on the remaining gifts. The non-charismatics preach against the miraculous gifts, and in turn, put little or no emphasis on the remaining gifts. Or, as one pastor stated, "So much of what is written is either in defense of the Charismatic position or an attack against it."

It appears that the trend is changing. The remaining gifts are the task oriented gifts or what I am calling the TEAM Gifts. Most leaders, regardless of their position, would agree that these are also the "Church Growth" oriented gifts as well. Therefore, I have limited this study to these TEAM Gifts for that reason.

Teaching the correct doctrinal position concerning the miraculous gifts is a must. There is much good material available to help you form a Biblical doctrinal position. Be careful in your selections. There is so much written on this subject, that regardless of any combination of thoughts you might come up with, you can find someone to agree with you. Without a doubt, the best book ever written on the subject is the Bible, and it is much clearer than you might think. Read I Corinthians 12, 13 and 14 first, and ask God to direct you.

The Enabling Gifts

The ENABLING Gifts are catalyst gifts that tie your spiritual qualities to your spiritual gifts. A catalyst is an agent which, when added, speeds up the process of the other agents. In other words, the Enabling Gifts speed up the process of using the TEAM Gifts, thereby making them more effective. The Enabling Gifts are available to all Christians and should be sought by all.

I will discuss the ENABLING Gifts at length in Chapter Five.

The TEAM Gifts

The third category of spiritual gifts is TEAM Gifts. They are job, activity or *task oriented* gifts. They are functional. The TEAM Gifts are then divided into two groups, *speaking* and *ministering* gifts. That is not to say you do not minister with the speaking gifts nor speak in the ministering gifts. In I Peter 4:9-11, Peter speaks of two groups in which to place the gifts. He says in verse 11, "If any man speak, let him speak as the oracles of God; if any man minister, let him do it as of the ability which God giveth." Therefore, Peter gives us two groups of the TEAM Gifts: (1) "speaking" (the Greek word *laleo*) means to talk, utter words. Those who have the speaking gifts are: Evangelist, Prophet, Teacher, Exhorter and Pastor-Teacher; (2) "ministering" — ministers are not kings but "king-makers". They are support gifts. They are people who are happy to work behind the scenes supporting the ones who have the "speaking" gifts. Ministering gifts include Pastor-Teacher, Mercy shower, Server, Giver and Administrator. Note that the Pastor-Teacher is on both lists. This is because of the many responsibilities God has given him as a shepherd.

A brief description, characteristics, strengths, weaknesses and some areas where people with the TEAM Gifts are often misunderstood are covered in Chapters Six, Seven and Eight. As you study them you need to understand they are generalized and there are as many variations and degrees as there are people who have these gifts. There is also a charted outline for each gift so that you can readily see the distinct characteristics of each gift.

CHAPTER FIVE

THE ENABLING GIFTS

It is Christmas Eve and the whole family is in bed except Dad. . .oops . . .Santa Claus. He's extremely busy on the floor of the den, putting together several gifts that require assembly before tomorrow morning. He carefully inserts tab A into slot B and adds glue to the edge of side C, then holds it onto side D until he can screw it together with screws (of course, both are labeled X). Soon he has two of the three assembling jobs finished. The last item should be a cinch. He had read the instructions of all three and had done the most difficult first so that he would not be up half the night.

He finishes about two-thirds of the last job and suddenly stops with a puzzled look on his face. He checks and double-checks the instructions. He looks around the floor and the end tables, growing more perplexed by the minute. He is missing a piece. The bearing assembly that allows all the moving parts of the toy to work is nowhere to be found.

After sitting in the middle of the mess for about three or four minutes, he hears a noise in the hallway that sounds like a mouse. Puzzled, he tiptoes to see what it is. The cat is playing with something metal and small. Dad starts back into the den with a chuckle when he realizes what he saw. The cat had found the bearing assembly. Dad becomes Santa again and grabs the assembly and puts it into the proper place in the new toy. Now the entire movement of the toy can take place and it can become totally operational.

The purpose of this material is to help the believer recognize and develop his or her TEAM Gifts, but it is necessary to recognize that the TEAM Gifts can never be fully operational in the absence of the ENABLING Gifts. Just as a catalyst in a chemistry experiment is an extra agent which speeds up or causes an action to take place (such as heat or pressure), the ENABLING Gifts are the third agent which is introduced to cause a spiritual task to be successfully performed.

The ENABLING Gifts of *faith, discernment, wisdom* and *knowledge* are qualities possessed rather than activities performed. (For example, knowledge is something you possess within you. Likewise, faith is something you possess within you. In contrast, the gift of teaching is an activity you perform.) The ENABLING Gifts provide a foundation for action. They do not describe what you do but rather what you are. The Holy Spirit reveals Himself to you through the ENABLING Gifts as you use your TEAM Gift.

The Holy Spirit reveals the qualities of the ENABLING Gifts to you and to others as you minister to their needs. For example, I once taught a series on creation. As I studied, the Holy Spirit revealed Himself and gave me more faith. This teaching strengthened my faith in Christ. This added faith was evident to my pupils as I taught them.

The Bible tells us how important the ENABLING Gift of faith is in the functioning of the TEAM Gifts. "Having then gifts differing according to the grace that is given to us, whether prophecy, let us prophesy according to the proportion of faith" (Romans 12:6). How can we prophesy? According to the measure of faith. How can I teach? According to the measure of faith. The more faith I have, the better teacher I will be. In turn, that makes the ENABLING Gifts the determining factor of the level of ability for the TEAM Gift that God has given me.

All Christians have the ability to develop the enabling gifts. Let's take the ENABLING Gifts one at a time and examine them.

FAITH: "For I say, through the grace given unto me, to every man that is among you, not to think of himself more highly than he ought to think; but to think soberly, according as God hath dealt to every man the measure of faith" (Romans 12:3). The Scripture clearly says that *every man* has a measure of faith. Every Christian has *stewardship faith.* The question comes, "Why, then, if every Christian has the gift of faith, can some Christians use this gift far beyond other Christians?" Some scholars seem to think, because of the wording which says "the measure of faith", the Scripture indicates that every one is given the same amount of faith. Why can't we operate on the faith of George Muller, the "man of faith"? He was able to raise several million dollars for the orphanages with no public appeal for money. He just prayed in needed funds. Why can't we do the same?

When a person is born, he has all the muscle tissue in his body he will ever have. Yet some people are non-muscular and pot-bellied, while others have broad shoulders and large muscles. What is the difference? The biggest difference is exercise. As we exercise our faith, it will grow and develop.

What would happen if we took a man who couldn't swim out in the middle of a lake and threw him out of the boat? Naturally, he would drown.

But, what if, before we took him out in the boat, we gave him hours of classroom education about the water and swimming (but we had never let him in the water) — what would happen then? He would still drown. He would just look a little better doing it.

Suppose we took another man who couldn't swim, put him in the water, and gave him some training. After we taught him to swim, we would have him swim 10 yards, then 20, and 30 yards. Before we knew it, he could swim the length of the pool 20 times non-stop. When we took him out to the middle of the lake — what would happen? He would beat the boat back. What was the difference? It was the training and the exercise. The same is true with the gift of faith. We first have to exercise our faith on small decisions. Usually we don't.

How can we learn to exercise more faith? Romans 10:17 says, "So then, faith cometh by hearing, and hearing by the word of God." This tells me that the amount of faith I have has a direct relationship to the amount of the Word of God I know. The best way to increase your faith is by increasing your knowledge of the Word of God.

I have noticed this: usually, people who have the gift of faith are "spiritual giants". These men and women are "supermen of faith". Most of them are leaders, and most of them are people with the gift of administration. However, they are men and women who are able to trust God for the little things as well as the big things.

Leslie Flynn, speaking of George Muller writes, "The possessor of the gift of faith will limit his asking to only those things that God wants. His desire will correspond with God's desire. Faith is firm conviction that God wishes to do something remarkable. Faith thinks big, it thinks the kind of big that God wants. Once he (George Muller) was persuaded that a thing was right, he went on praying for it until the answer came. He said, 'I never give up. Tens of thousands of times have my prayers been answered.' A stickler for detail, he kept a complete record of prayers that covered 3000 pages, contained nearly a million words, a chronicle of fifty thousand specific answers."[1] Again Flynn writes, "The gift of faith is often related to the gifts of governments or administration which grants prophetic leadership for planning of the future program."[2]

Many people today do not operate on the gift of faith. They make decisions based on circumstances, or they make "faith deals" with God.

Several years ago my wife and I decided to sell our business and home and go to school. It was a major decision for us. We made a "faith deal" with God. "Lord, if You want us to go away, You will find a buyer for our home within 90 days. If You do that, we will know that You want us to move. If You don't, we'll know You want us to stay." It sounded like a reasonable deal because the house had been appraised for considerably more than the asking price, and real estate was selling reasonably well at the time. But as the deadline grew nearer, we became more and more miserable. We were under the conviction we had made a wrong decision in offering such a deal. We then decided that we were going to move regardless of what happened. The only thing that would stop us was God putting a stone wall in front of us. We left and three months after I was in school, we sold our home. My wife and I have not doubted for one minute that God wanted us to move. We didn't make the wrong decision. We did make a wrong choice in the way we decided to move.

When God and you both know you are going to stick to a decision regardless of what happens, then (and only then) can you operate on the faith you have instead of the faith you wish you had.

Discernment: Harold Willmington gives a wonderful illustration that can explain the gift of discernment. He said he was in a bank one day talking to the banker and he said, "You must have an awful lot of problems with counterfeit money."

The banker replied, "On the contrary, we have no problem at all. Our clerks can spot it right off."

"That looks like it would take a lot of training to teach people to spot counterfeit money."

"Not really", replied the banker. "All we do is send the clerks down to the Federal Reserve Bank where they work for two weeks doing nothing but counting money. The problem with counterfeit money is not the printing. With the printing equipment they have today, they can do almost foolproof printing. The problem is always the paper. With our clerks handling all this paper, they learn the real thing so well that when a counterfeit goes through their hands, without even looking down, they can pull it out." They do it by learning the real thing. This is discernment. How do you learn discernment? By learning the real thing. Today we are seeing Christians leaving Bible-believing works and joining the Moonies, the Mormons, or a variety of other cults. We are not teaching them the discernment they need to recognize the real thing from the counterfeit.

What is discernment? It is the ability to distinguish, particularly as it pertains to what is real and what is false. It is also gives one the ability to set priorities based on what is good, what is better and what is best. There are so many areas in our modern society that require discernment on the part of the believer. Many situations we face today are not boldly black and white. Technologies, knowledge and time factors often do not allow us the luxury of time to determine all the facts we need for making good solid decisions with the "mind of Christ". Yet, very little is said in the pulpit and by Christian writers about the gift of discernment. We must be encouraged to develop the gift of discernment. It is an area which requires the Holy Spirit's control and leadership in our thinking processes.

Wisdom: is a combination of honesty and knowledge applied through experience. It is also one of the gifts that will enable you to perform your TEAM Gift more effectively.

A bank clerk was to be promoted to president. The current president, the founder, was 75 years old. Before the older gentleman retired, the young clerk went to see him. He said, "Sir, you have built this bank from a little corner bank of years ago to 35 branch offices in six counties. I wonder if, before you retire, you could give me some advice as to how you did it?"

"Sure," he said, "it all boils down to two words — *right decisions.*"

The clerk thought for a few seconds and said, "That's good advice, Sir. But how does one go about making right decisions?"

The old gentleman replied, "One word — *experience.*"

The clerk thought another moment and said, "That's good advice too, but how does one go about getting experience?"

"Two words," replied the old man, "*wrong decisions.*"

According to James, "If any of you lack wisdom, let him ask of God, that giveth to all men liberally, and upbraideth not; and it shall be given him. But let him ask in faith, nothing wavering" (James 1:5-6). Note the condition about asking in faith without wavering. This refers to more than persevering in prayer. When God is giving us wisdom, He often passes us through situations where we must stretch the wisdom we already have. It is much like the banker noted earlier. We must often make bad decisions in order to learn how to make good decisions. God does not suddenly give us supernatural wisdom. It is like all the other ENABLING and TEAM Gifts. It must be exercised in order to become stronger.

In the context of James 1, this truth becomes even more evident. In verses 3 and 4 he says, "The trying of your faith worketh patience. Let patience have her perfect work, that you may be perfect and entire, wanting nothing." We must have "trials by fire" to obtain patience and wisdom.

This promise of wisdom, like many promises in the Bible, is conditional. In order to claim the promise, you must have exceptional faith. "But let him ask in faith, nothing wavering. For he that wavereth is like a wave of the sea driven with the wind and tossed. For let not that man think that he shall receive anything of the Lord" (James 1:6-7). This passage indicates the amount of your wisdom is determined by the amount of your faith.

When you ask for wisdom, believe unwaveringly that God will give it to you as you exercise the little amount of wisdom you have now.

Knowledge and wisdom go hand in hand. In reviewing our lives, much of our wisdom has come from the simple fact that we have made wrong decisions.

Knowledge: This ENABLING Gift is best characterized in Proverbs 2:1-5. "My son, if thou wilt receive my words, and hide my commandments with thee; So that thou incline thine ear unto wisdom, and apply thine heart to understanding; Yea, if thou criest after knowledge, and lifteth up thy voice for understanding; If thou seekest her as silver, and searchest for her as for hid treasures; Then shalt thou understand the fear of the Lord, and find the knowledge of God." Again, note the conditions. Knowledge, like wisdom, is contingent on meeting conditions. How does the world seek silver? If a man thought he had hidden treasure in his back yard, he would dig up his whole back yard seeking this treasure. Of course, the question is, "Where do we seek and where do we dig to find this silver and this treasure?" The word of God is the place to dig for wisdom and knowledge.

Make no mistake, this seeking requires time, faith, patience and perserverance. There is far too much to learn to expect instant results. The entire life is spent in learning new facts. A friend of mine told me of a Deacon in a church he pastored. The man was in his seventies. He refused to be taught anything new that would change his thinking. He felt that since he had spent so many years experiencing life that a younger man couldn't teach him anything. It was soon evident that the man's spiritual life was becoming stagnant with no excitement or challenge. It was strictly status quo as far as he was concerned. The sad fact is, many younger folks have the same problem.

When we quit learning, we quit living. The Christian should be constantly and consistently eager to learn and hungry for more knowledge. It would even be worth many hard hours of tedious study to have more knowledge.

Now What?

As stated earlier, the ENABLING Gifts are CATALYST gifts. They are the gifts that accelerate and empower the use of the TEAM Gifts. The Enabling Gifts are more character than performance. The stronger they are made in the life of the believer, the better the TEAM Gifts will be performed. Every Christian should strive to strengthen the Enabling Gifts. In so doing, he will be aiding in the development of his TEAM Gifts which are developed in two way: (1) using the gift in a task or ministry and developing that task; (2) strengthening the ENABLING Gifts which in turn strengthen a believer's maturity.

FOOTNOTES:

[1]   Flynn, Leslie, *19 Gifts of the Spirit* (Victor Books: Wheaton, 1978) Page 142.
[2]   Ibid, page 144.

INTRODUCTION AND CHAPTER FIVE

REVIEW QUESTIONS:

1. What are the four positions on the MIRACULOUS or Charismatic gifts? What is your church's position?

2. What are the ENABLING Gifts?

3. Name a Bible character who had great faith; discernment; wisdom; knowledge.

DISCUSSION QUESTIONS:

1. Why are the ENABLING Gifts called the catalyst gifts? How can they help the other gifts?

2. What kind of barriers do Christians encounter in developing the ENABLING Gifts and how can they overcome them? Which are the most difficult to overcome?

3. If the ENABLING Gifts are available to every Christian, why do you think they are not evident in some?

CHAPTER SIX

THE EVANGELIST, THE PROPHET, THE TEACHER

It is important to understand that the next three chapters explain the general characteristics, strengths and weaknesses of the TEAM Gifts. These characteristics are general observations and the product of research which has taken place for over ten years on my part. Part of that research has been studying other authors on the subject of spiritual gifts, as well as discussions with and oberservation of those who have these various gifts. The following explanations and the outlines typify certain gifts in the lives of various individuals who possess those gifts. Some are full-time ministers and others are laymen.

There is no claim to divine inspiration, nor do the lists come from the Bible. They are simply intended as a tool to help you determine your own gift and to recognize other gifted individuals.

It would be wise to study these chapters at least twice: once for the purpose of understanding your own gift and again for the purpose of understanding other believers so that you can love them and work with them as a TEAM.

The Evangelist

The Greek word *Euange-listes* means to proclaim glad tidings, a messenger of good. It denotes a preacher or proclaimer of the gospel.

The EVANGELIST can either be a preacher who stands before a crowd imploring them to be saved, or perhaps an individual sitting across from someone pleading for him to accept Christ in his living room or on a plane.

The person with the gift of evangelism usually is outgoing and personable. He has mastered a technique of paying compliments to every stranger and asking questions about his lifestyle, such as where he works, how many children he has or the part of the country where he was raised. When not talking with people about their soul's relationship with Jesus Christ, he is often quiet and keeps to himself.

The evangelist is constantly consumed with the need of confronting sinners with the gospel or encouraging other Christians to do the same. He does this either by directly telling them to do so, or encouraging them by telling about his own most recent experience. Scripture is quoted often since he has memorized much of it in order not to be caught "flat-footed" while witnessing.

Sometimes he turns off other Christians and even lost people because of his "sales pitch". Some consider him kin to the used car salesman or vacuum cleaner salesman. However, most of that problem is caused by how others view him rather than his own motives or desires.

The definition of the evangelist as found in the Greek is an indication of the ministry of any person who has the gift of evangelism. The confrontational witness (some prefer the term soul-winner) is not limited by lack of opportunities, but makes opportunities for himself. The definition offered by some that the evangelist is a church planting gift limits the scope of the gift. That definition probably has become popular because of the fact that most church planters have the gift of evangelism and it fits the task of outreach and saturation evangelism needed to successfully begin a new work. Church growth in any type of church probably has at least one gifted evangelist involved at the center of outreach, regardless of the church's age or size.

Because of the importance of outreach in the church, God has given two ways to evangelize a lost world. First, He gives every Christian the role of witness. Secondly, He gives some Christians (approximately 10% — see Chapter Eleven) the gift of evangelism. It is important that the difference between the two is understood. This will be discussed more fully later (Chapter Eleven).

Spiritual Maturity In The Evangelist Equals Credibility In His Witness.

Philip is the only evangelist identified clearly in Scripture (Acts 21:8). He was also one of the first deacons (Acts 6:3-5). As such, he met the qualifications of a deacon (I Timothy 3:8-12; Titus 1:6-8). Note what kind of man God chose as His evangelist. He was a man with no *obvious problems* in his life. Not only must the evangelist win souls, but he must also live in such a manner as not to bring reproach upon his message.

Most evangelists will probably influence 30 people to every one he wins, many times leaving the other 29 for someone else to harvest. But if he falls spiritually, he takes his 29 onlookers down with him. Many aggressive soul-winners have done more harm for the cause of Christ than they have done good. For this reason, if for no other, it is important that those with the gift of Evangelism receive the proper training to help them become spiritually mature and a more effective evangelist.

Many new Christians are almost forced to win souls. Sometimes he is thrust into a situation he is not yet equipped to handle. Before giving him a full responsibility to be a confrontational soul-winner, he should be brought to some maturity in his Christian walk. This would keep a young Christian with some areas that need correcting from hurting his witness before those who do not know his past and have not seen the changes in his life.

However, his enthusiasm as a new Christian anxious to share his new-found faith should not be wasted. If I were a pastor, I would want to have the excited new convert providing prospects and giving testimony to those whom he knew before he was saved, but I would not want him being the salesman. In other words, he knows people who are without Christ and have seen the changes that have taken place in his life by receiving Christ as Savior. He has an open opportunity to say, "Look what the Lord has done for me." But he may not be ready to go into a stranger's home and present Christ if he has areas that still need changing.

The solution is to have the young Christian go visiting with a seasoned, mature Christian who has the gift of evangelism. He will learn much about presenting the gospel by watching that evangelist minister to the lost.

THE EVANGELIST

The Spirit-given capacity and desire to serve God by leading people, beyond his natural sphere of influence, to the saving knowledge of Jesus Christ.
The aggressive soul-winner who seeks the lost.

I. CHARACTERISTICS

A. He is outgoing and seldom meets a stranger.
B. He is well groomed and neatly dressed.
C. He usually keeps to himself in personal times.
D. He feels fulfilled working one-on-one or with groups.
E. He is active socially, gets along well with others.
F. He is more lighthearted than depressed.
G. He is expressive in speech and communication.
H. He is subjective rather than objective in viewing things.
I. He is tolerant of people and their weaknesses; sympathetic to sinners.
J. He is impulsive at times, not usually self-disciplined; likely to make decisions based on emotions.
K. He appears peaceable and agreeable.
L. He displays enthusiasm.
M. He is talkative and often interrupts people.
N. He enjoys being center stage and having everybody looking at him.

II. BURDENS, DESIRES AND STRENGTHS

A. He has a consuming passion for lost souls.
B. He believes salvation is the greatest gift of all.
C. He has a desire to meet lost people.
D. He would rather confront the lost with the gospel than anything else.
E. He is forgiving.
F. He has a clear understanding of the gospel message.
G. He usually has a burden to memorize Scripture.
H. He has a great joy in seeing men and women come to Christ.
I. He demonstrates an air of competence.

    J. He holds the attention of the listener.
    K. He remembers people's names and faces.
    L. He works hard to become a good listener.

III. SPECIAL NEEDS AND WEAKNESSES

    A. He thinks everybody should be "evangelists".
    B. He may be satisfied to get a decision just to get one.
    C. He may turn people off by pressing for a decision.
    D. He rarely will admit that evangelism (as soul-winning) is a gift. He usually has another definition for evangelist.
    E. He believes strongly in "confrontation evangelism".
    F. He tends to dominate other people.
    G. He thinks every message must be an attempt to win the lost. This usually causes him to be weak on teaching other areas of Scripture.

IV. HOW HE IS MISUNDERSTOOD BY OTHERS

    A. Others think he is not interested in other church programs.
    B. Others think he is pushy.
    C. Others think his aggressiveness is for his own benefit.
    D. Others think he is more interested in numbers than people.
    E. Others think he judges their spirituality by the number of souls they have won.

V. HOW SATAN ATTACKS THIS GIFT

    A. Causes pride in number of "converts".
    B. Causes failure to grow and learn.
    C. Causes him to see people as numbers rather than people with needs.
    D. Causes discouragement when converts are few or infrequent.
    E. Causes lack of concern for Bible passages that can't be used as "soul-winning texts".

VI. WHERE TO USE THIS GIFT

A. In visitation programs.
B. In special evangelistic efforts, such as fairs, etc.
C. In altar call or invitation to lead new converts to Christ.
D. In church planting.
E. In Gospel Teams.
F. In migrant ministry.
G. In many public preaching ministries.

The Prophet

The Greek word *Prophet-eria* means to speak forth the mind and the counsel of God.

Some believe the Old Testament prophet and the New Testament prophet are not the same, but a close study will show that there is great similarity. The Old Testament prophets are often viewed as only *fore-tellers*. But in reality they spent more time as *forthtellers*, warning Israel and other people to repent of their wickedness and turn to God. This is also the theme of the New Testament prophet. He is a *forthteller* , telling the mind of God. Before the completion of the New Testament, prophets would receive their revelation directly from God. Now that the Bible is complete, he gets the truths and principles directly from God by reading and studying God's Word. He then applies God's standard to the culture and lifestyle around him.

The gift of prophecy is basically the gift of preaching. But note that the gift seems to carry with it the need for a special kind of preaching. The prophet is the hell-fire, brimstone preacher that points out sin, and when people with sin in their lives respond in repentance, his preaching results in edification, exhortation and comfort (see I Corinthians 14:3).

Every Christian has a need to become aware of the sin in his or her life. When there is unconfessed sin, one cannot walk with God as he should. This is where the prophet's ministry takes place. He is the person who speaks the mind and counsel of God concerning sin and righteousness. He points out sin, usually from the pulpit as a hell-fire brimstone preacher, although the prophet is not always found in full-time Christian service.

The PROPHETS are the Ralph Naders of Christianity. They have the ability to see that which is wrong. A prophet can walk into a room and immediately see six things wrong but has to concentrate for a while in order to see something right.

However, the prophet usually spends much time praying and weeping over the sins of the church and for lost sinners. He carries a great burden constantly over the sinful condition of the world around him. At every opportunity he will proclaim that everyone must "repent or perish".

Churches and Christians need to be exposed to the prophets and their preaching. Those who are not periodically exposed to the prophet's preaching will generally lean toward worldliness and the flesh. There will be a lack of conviction concerning their sinfulness.

Most real revivals begin in prayer meetings, but have a prophet as the front man, making the church aware of sin and challenging people to be burdened for their community or church by praying and confessing their sins. Consequently, God visits His people in power and more conviction by the Holy Spirit and the fire begins to spread until a spiritual awakening takes place. It all starts and will continue to grow because of the faithfulness of a prophet pointing out sin and the need for repentance.

How Do You View The Prophet?

Possibly the most dominant problem with the prophet's ministry is not caused by the prophet but rather by how others view his ministry.

Do you view the prophet with an *open* mind or a *closed* mind? Do you accept, reject or rebel at what the prophet is saying? I have seen classes and services where some people sat and listened with three ears while others were getting red in the face. The difference was one group was open-minded and the other closed. If you are rebelling or rejecting the teacher or preacher because his messages are convicting you, the problem is with you, not the teacher or the teaching.

Open Minded: Very often a person with an open mind can become very uncomfortable sitting under the preaching of a prophet. It hurts, but he is willing to do something about it. The next time the preacher preaches, he's back listening.

Closed Minded: This is a very serious position to be in because if you are closed minded, you will never grow. *You are as good a Christian today as you will ever be. You are as Christlike as you will ever be.*

Since so many Christians are closed minded to the prophet's preaching, many prophets are forced to become traveling evangelists, holding revival meetings in churches, in order to exist in the ministry. (This is not to imply that all traveling evangelists have that reason for their ministry.) The harshness of the prophet's message makes it difficult for him to pastor a church for any length of time. The exceptions are: (1) when he is able to temper his harsh message with a loving spirit and possibly has the gift of pastor-teacher as well as prophecy; and (2) when he is able to gravitate around many others with the gift of prophecy (colonization). This will usually be a legalistic ministry.

One of the biggest challenges for the prophet is to keep a spirit of love, especially in relationship to his family. When a prophet keeps a tender loving heart, he will be a blessing to his home, his church and to individual believers, making a real impact on their spirituality. In order to do this, he must always be "speaking the truth in love" (Ephesians 4:15).

THE PROPHET

The Spirit-given capacity and desire to serve God by proclaiming God's truth.
The hell-fire-brimstone preacher who points out sin.

I. CHARACTERISTICS

A. He is not very patient, especially with people and their problems.
B. He is disorganized and depends on others to keep him on schedule.
C. He is very discerning.
D. He is usually much more pleasant when not speaking or preaching.
E. He has a strong self-image and is individualistic.
F. He has a strong sense of duty, not caring what others think about what he does because of it.
G. He is very opinionated.
H. He is more likely to be depressed and serious than lighthearted about life.
I. He desires to be alone frequently.
J. He is not usually inhibited, but is usually expressive.
K. He will be more interested in his own aims and desires than others'.
L. He is more likely to be authoritative, especially about Scriptures.
M. He will be dominant, not submissive.

II. BURDENS, DESIRES AND STRENGTHS

A. He is burdened to expose sin in others.
B. He must preach. He wouldn't be content just writing.
C. He wants to make all the "softies" in the church stronger.
D. He speaks with urgency and presses for rapid decisions.
E. He desires to see a world without sin. He wants to see revival.
F. He wants to stir your conscience.
G. He preaches for conviction.
H. He enjoys speaking publicly and does it with boldness.
I. He is more likely to be hostile than tolerant, especially about sin.
J. He is usually a disciplinarian. He wants things done right.
K. He is able to make quick decisions; is seldom indecisive.

L. He is sometimes less discerning than he believes he is.

M. He sees problems where others do not.

N. He is idealistic.

III. SPECIAL NEEDS AND WEAKNESSES

A. He doesn't like to study. He relies on others to do his background work. He has a poor memory for details.

B. He doesn't relate well one-on-one. He doesn't worry about being gracious.

C. He over-categorizes. Mostly, sometimes, often, 80% are not words from his vocabulary. He replaces them with "all".

D. He tries to convict rather than letting the Spirit convict.

E. He judges others quickly.

F. He jumps to conclusions and makes decisions before all the facts are available to him. He does not analyze the details.

G. He tends to look at the negative side of things.

H. He does not make or follow through with long-range goals and plans.

I. He tends to be selfish.

J. He uses sarcasm and teasing to get his point across, is not tactful.

K. He is bossy and impatient. He has little tolerance for mistakes. He wants things done *his* way *now*.

L. He is likely to stir up trouble.

M. He is cautious about making friends. He is suspicious by nature.

N. He is able to hold the audience's attention.

IV. HOW HE IS MISUNDERSTOOD BY OTHERS

A. Others think he is not understanding.

B. Others think he looks at a congregation as all bad.

C. Others think he makes some people doubt their salvation.

D. Others think he is insensitive and cold and has no love for people.

E. Others think he is a poor listener.

F. Others think he is too self-disciplined and can't have a good time.

G. Others think he receives joy in hurting the feelings of others.

H. Others think he is too demanding.

V. HOW SATAN ATTACKS THIS GIFT

A. Causes lack of compassion.
B. Causes pride and self-righteousness over lack of certain sins.
C. Causes anger and bitterness.
D. Causes lack of forgiveness.
E. Causes discouragement because of unrepentant attitude by others.
F. Causes him to sometimes fall into the very sins he preaches against.
G. Causes him to never say, "I'm sorry."
H. Causes a pessimistic attitude.

VI. WHERE TO USE THIS GIFT

A. In revival speaking.
B. In pastoring when he has other gifts suitable for pastoring.
C. In problem-solving for a church with a sin problem.
D. In counselling to help point out sin in person's life.
E. In preaching on Gospel Teams.
F. In prison ministry.
G. In migrant ministry.

The Teacher

The Greek word for teacher, *didaskalos* means master, teacher or doctor. The teacher is one who communicates knowledge, guides, makes known or relays facts.

The person with the gift of teaching is not the person we often think of as a teacher in the Sunday School class. The TEACHER to whom I refer is the scholar, the person who learns and teaches with more depth than the average Sunday School teacher.

There are two areas for which the teacher lives: learning and teaching (or writing if he teaches through the written medium). He would rather gain knowledge than to eat, sleep or just about anything else.

The teacher must learn to teach in two manners which are contrary to his or her nature. First, the material must be kept simple so that students can understand it. The students normally do not have the hunger for knowledge that the person with the gift of teaching has. Secondly, it must be kept practical, for the teacher will love knowledge whether it is in practical form or not. The most effective teacher is the one who can teach more than average knowledge with more than average simplicity.

Many churches will not have a teacher at all while others may have only one or two, depending on their community and church needs. Most teachers (scholars) will be found in full time Christian vocations. The teaching gift will involve the lowest number of laymen (in its scholarly sense). The most common place to find the believer with the gift of teaching is in a church with a Bible Institute program, a Christian college or one which is near a publishing house for Christian literature.

We must have our gifted teachers to handle the interpretation problems, deeper theology and to teach those with the other teaching gifts in a more complete manner. People with the gift of teaching do not necessarily have to teach the Bible to be a help to the church ministry. The teaching in such areas as education, business and finance or computers for example may be of great benefit in some churches.

It must be remembered that the scholarly teacher is only one of four teaching or communication gifts. The other three, the pastor-teacher, the prophet and the exhorter usually have to rely on resources from the teacher in order to fulfill their responsibilities in the local church.

The problems that are seen most often in connection with the teaching gift are those created by believers who have desires in other areas and find the teacher to be dull or too deep for their liking. The blessing is that the teacher (scholar) can challenge us to learn more rather than being complacent with what knowledge we think we already have.

Most teacher's aid books, reference books and commentaries are written by people with the gift of teaching.

THE TEACHER

The Spirit-given capacity and desire to serve God by making clear the truth of the Word of God with accuracy and simplicity.
The scholar making clear the doctrine and teachings of the Bible.

I. CHARACTERISTICS

A. He has a love for the Word.
B. He usually enjoys reading.
C. He is not usually an extrovert and may be a little shy of strangers.
D. He prefers groups over individuals when teaching.
E. He is creative and imaginative.
F. He is usually confident in his drive to accomplish; accurate self-image.
G. He is generally self-disciplined.
H. He sometimes is technical; usually methodical.
I. He is genius-prone.
J. He loves charts, graphs and lists.

II. BURDENS, DESIRES AND STRENGTHS

A. He has a great burden to know and teach the whole Bible.
B. He relies highly upon the authority of the Scriptures.
C. He has an organized system to store facts.
D. He would sometimes rather just do research, but "must teach" because others would not teach it the way he would.
E. The use of a verse out of context upsets him.
F. He will question the knowledge of those who teach him.
G. He puts a great importance on education.
H. He is an accumulator of knowledge and is analytical.
I. He is usually objective in making decisions, based on facts not feelings.
J. He enjoys studying for long periods of time. He likes it quiet, needs time to think.
K. He likes to see things clearly and always looking for better ways to communicate truth.

L. He is enthusiastic when explaining; stimulates others to learn; easily understood when teaching.
M. He is always concerned with accuracy, often dwelling on the trivial.

III. SPECIAL NEEDS AND WEAKNESSES

A. He tends to be critical of those who differ with his doctrine.
B. He puts great emphasis on word usage and pronunciation.
C. He tends to measure others' spirituality by the amount of their Bible knowledge.
D. He finds other people's material hard to present.
E. He finds practical application hard to present.
F. He can have a small need for relationships with people. He sometimes needs people only as an audience.
G. He is more likely to talk than to listen.
H. He needs to see a positive response from his students.
I. He may have a narrow field of interest.
J. He can easily spend more time studying than actually teaching.
K. He usually makes friends cautiously.
L. He has little tolerance for mistakes.
M. He reads directions only when all else fails.

IV. HOW HE IS MISUNDERSTOOD BY OTHERS

A. Others think he is a poor counselor.
B. Others think he gives too many details.
C. Others think he is more interested in presenting facts than he is in his students.
D. Others think he doesn't have time for them.
E. Others often think he is boring.

V. HOW SATAN ATTACKS THIS GIFT

A. Causes pride and feeling of superiority because of his knowledge. This is reinforced when others consider him a final authority.
B. Causes him to lose sight of people's needs.

C. Causes discouragement and disenchantment because of others' lack of interest.
D. Causes lack of zeal.

VI. WHERE TO USE THIS GIFT

A. As a teacher of teachers.
B. As a writer and developer of curriculum.
C. As a Bible College or Seminary teacher.
D. As a Bible Institute teacher in local church.
E. As a Missionary-teacher.
F. As a correspondence course instructor.

CHAPTER SIX

REVIEW QUESTIONS:

1. Give the definition of the Greek word "Euangelistes".

2. What is the most important thing in the life of the prophet?

3. How many times does the word *evangelist* appear in the Bible and who is the only person who is called an evangelist?

DISCUSSION QUESTIONS:

1. Have you seen negative reactions to the evangelists and prophets (no names please)? What kind? How could those reactions be minimized by the evangelist and prophet?

2. Does the fact that not everyone has the gift of evangelism change the responsibility of the individual to be a witness? How?

3. How can a person with the gift of teaching work with people with the various gifts in order to be most effective in his or her teaching? What part do you think variety plays in teaching methodology?

CHAPTER SEVEN

THE EXHORTER, THE PASTOR/SHEPHERD, THE MERCY SHOWER

Exhorter

The Greek word *Parakaleo* means to admonish, to encourage, to beseech. The exhorter is a "how to" man. Everything he teaches revolves around telling people "how to do it". Although the gift of exhortation has a different motivation than the gift of teaching, it should still be thought of as a *teaching* gift.

EXHORTERS often make the best counselors, because they are willing to spend time with people and give them the practical steps they need to solve their problems. They also can see the big picture — from problem to solution.

He is a person of practical application, yet very result oriented. Everything the exhorter wants to do and does must be done on a very practical basis. He's not very interested in theology or doctrine. He wants the practical aspects of the Scriptures, to teach man how to solve his problems, and how to make the necessary changes to be a more mature Christian. (Of course, he wishes to be doctrinally sound, but that is not his emphasis.) He has a strong belief that God's word has the answer for every problem.

The exhorter has a step for everything. If you go to him with a problem, he might say, "Here, do a, b, c, and come back next week, and I will give you d, e, and f and then the next week..." The exhorter is a very simplified person and he does not like a lot of details. He just gives enough detail to get the job done.

Exhorters often end up teaching seminars for Christian workers, helping them achieve more in their ministries. They also make excellent teachers in Bible colleges or seminaries in the area of practical methodology.

The exhorter is also a person of encouragement. Synonyms for exhort include such words as admonish, persuade, instigate, urge and appeal. These words carry a sense of urgency. When the exhorter instructs how to live and how to solve problems or to carry out God's work, he usually is also encouraging the listener to "get with it" and put the plan to work.

There is also an aspect of the gift which involves what is commonly called motivation. True motivation comes from within a person, but the exhorter is usually able to trigger that inner motivation through encouragement, excitement and enthusiasm. The exhorter is usually more interested in the positive than the negative. He seldom uses "Thou shalt not" as a way to get people to act, but he uses ideas and methods which will make the right way seem better to that person than the wrong way; or he is able to make the right way more exciting and more practical. He is the encourager and cheerleader of the TEAM.

Some people think the exhorter makes things too simple and that he sometimes skips over essential details; some things are just too complicated to work his way. If he is a pastor, evangelist or teacher, he often is accused of not using enough Scripture or stretching it out of context to meet his purpose. They also resent his organized plans and would rather just "let things happen" rather than adhere strictly to his plans. Besides, he wants to accomplish too much too fast as far as they are concerned. After all, he has a thousand goals and ideas and a solution or program for everything. Sometimes he has difficulty translating all his ideas into action.

The Exhorter's Approach to Teaching

His goal is to present material that will enable the Holy Spirit to promote change in the student's life. The responsibility of people with the teaching gifts is to take a man who was lost and help him to become mature in Christ, not just have class participation or meaningful discussions. Many teachers become bogged down with using these good teaching methods and making them the primary goals for the class.

The exhorter uses Scripture as it applies to everyday living, not just Bible stories or Bible facts. Many teachers are guilty of teaching the Bible as a storybook. People know all about Jonah and the whale and the Garden of Eden; they can give you all the dimensions of the ark, but when it comes to making life decisions they don't know how to apply their knowledge. The exhorter teaches the Bible not just to answer Bible quizzes on Sunday night, but to answer life on Wednesday morning and Tuesday evening and so on.

Practical application is not prophecy (fore-telling). It has greatly concerned me to see the number of Christians who feed themselves on things which offer them limited growth at a time when they are open to learning the most. Ask a new Christian what he is reading besides the Bible and he will usually respond by referring to popular books on prophecy or some other book that has nothing to do with spiritual growth or Christian living. He needs to have basic practical Christian living taught to him. This is where the exhorter helps, by giving practical application to God's word and helping put the principles into practice. Prophecy can challenge the Christian into living right. The exhorter can explain in a practical way how to live right and encourage the person to continue practicing those practical things.

THE EXHORTER

The Spirit-given capacity and desire to serve God by motivating others to action by urging them to pursue a course of conduct.
The "HOW TO" teacher, giving the application of God's Word.

I. CHARACTERISTICS

A. He is result oriented.
B. He is comfortable working one-on-one or in groups.
C. He is a very practical person, usually analytical.
D. He is usually a good counsellor.
E. He is expressive in a group setting; group listens when he speaks.
F. He is usually impulsive, needs self-discipline.
G. He is more tolerant than hostile toward people, usually sympathetic.
H. He is accurate in his self-image.
I. He is serious minded, conservative, logical.
J. He is talkative.
K. He is an orderly person, likes things done in an orderly fashion.
L. He is enthusiastic, usually cheerful and bubbly.
M. He is a person of charts, graphs and lists.
N. He is bored with trivia.

II. BURDENS, DESIRES AND STRENGTHS

A. He is able to help others find their problems and solutions.
B. He shows interest mostly in the practical areas in studying the Scriptures.
C. He is burdened to show how Scripture relates to conduct.
D. He has a desire to unify people by using practical rather than doctrinal issues.
E. He puts great importance on the will of God.
F. He has several steps of action to solve every problem.
G. He has the ability to motivate others to action.
H. His messages are usually topical when preaching and teaching.
I. He is objective and makes decisions logically rather than on feelings.

J. He wants to see everyone reaching full potential.
K. He believes the Scripture has the solution to every problem.
L. He is a positive thinker, a strong believer that things will be better tomorrow.
M. He prefers the analysis to the task itself.
N. He occasionally needs to be alone where it's quiet in order to think.
O. He is extremely creative.
P. He likes being the center of attention.
Q. He outwardly demonstrates competence.

III. SPECIAL NEEDS AND WEAKNESSES

A. He may question the value of deep doctrinal studies.
B. He may have difficulty accepting himself because of the need of being an example.
C. He may be guilty of using Scripture only to support what he is teaching rather than starting with the Scriptures.
D. He is upset with impractical teaching.
E. He often interrupts other people because of his enthusiasm.
F. He enjoys motivating people to do more, do better and do their best.

IV. HOW HE IS MISUNDERSTOOD BY OTHERS

A. Others think he is not evangelistic.
B. Others think he makes everything too simple.
C. Others think he takes Scripture out of context just to suit his purpose.
D. Others think he doesn't use enough Scripture.
E. Others think he puts too much emphasis on edification.
F. Others think he is too positive when things look bleak.

V. HOW SATAN ATTACKS THIS GIFT

A. Causes pride in his motivational abilities.
B. Causes him to lose sight of people because of program emphasis.
C. Causes discouragement when results are not evident.

D. Causes him to encourage others to do the wrong thing because of his persuasive abilities.

VI. WHERE TO USE THIS GIFT

A. As a "trainer" in areas of leadership or methodology.
B. As a counsellor, especially in a counselling center.
C. As a "Church Training" teacher.
D. As a seminar speaker.
E. As a telephone ministry worker.
F. As a teacher of pre-marital classes.
G. As a counsellor in drug program, rescue mission, poverty program.
G. As a counsellor in half-way house and runaway ministry.
H. As a follow-up with new converts.
I. As a encourager with those who are discouraged.

The Pastor/Shepherd

The Greek word for pastor is *poimen*. In Ephesians 4:11, where Paul is listing spiritual gifts, this term is translated "pastor." The word *poimen* is translated pastor only one time in all of Scripture; however, it is used sixteen additional times. The remaining sixteen times are all translated "shepherd." Therefore, we must recognize that although Scripture uses the term pastor in this one instance, we are discussing the *gift* of shepherding, not the *position* of pastor. Though the pastor must have the gift of shepherding, everyone who has the gift of shepherding does not have the position of pastor. This gift can be utilized in many positions in the church other than senior pastor. The term shepherd and pastor or pastor/teacher can be used interchangeably, as the author has done throughout this material.

The shepherd leads and feeds, guards and protects, and oversees his flock. He is the coach or leader of the "team." The main thing on his mind is the welfare of those in his care. They are his sheep and he is their shepherd. He works under a pastor and is therefore an extension of the pastor and must "oversee" his part of the flock.

The shepherd/pastor-teacher is not a "jack of all and master of *none*," but a "jack of all and master of *one*." My experience has been that when this gift is used in the pastorate, the individual probably has another dominant speaking gift in his life besides the gift of shepherd. Although many are strong evangelists or teachers, or even exhorters, most pastors of large churches have dominant the gift of administration. However, the shepherd/pastor-teacher's heartbeat is shepherding the flock that God has given him while this other dominant gift complements his other ministry.

Ephesians 4 suggests that if anyone is given the gift of pastor/shepherd, then he must have the gift of teaching also. If you are sure you do not have a teaching gift, then you can be sure God has not given you the gift of pastor/shepherd or called you to the pastorate.

Women and the Gift of Shepherd

What may surprise some is the fact that more women exercise this gift than men. (Remember, we are talking about the gift of shepherd, not the office of pastor-teacher.) These women shepherds can exercise their gifts under the guidelines of Scripture by serving as Sunday School teachers of children or women. They can also be den mothers, dorm mothers at the local college, or leaders of support groups for troubled girls.

A Sunday School teacher (man or woman) is a shepherd the same as the pastor is a shepherd. Sunday School teachers are really pastoring small churches within a church. Their responsibility is to shepherd the class members. The position demands the gift.

First Corinthians 12:11 says that when God gives gifts, He divides "to every man severally as He will." Severally means according to one's own ability. God gives the gift of shepherd and puts one in a position where he can function according to his God-given ability. Some may have the ability to care for ten people, thus utilizing their gift in a capacity such as a Sunday School teacher. On the other hand, God may give someone else the ability to care for hundreds, therefore, allowing them to utilize their gift in the position of pastor.

Acts 14:23 ("And when they had ordained them elders in every church") indicates that more than one elder is to be appointed in the church. First Timothy 15:17 ("Let the elders that rule well be counted worthy of double honor, especially them who labor in the word and doctrine") indicates that the elders had different ranks, or junior and senior elders. Who are these junior elders of pastors? *Sunday School teachers.* When Luke penned Acts 14:23, the Sunday School was not in existence. If it had been, the verse may have read, "And they ordained pastors and Sunday School teachers in every church."

Most women test high in this gift because their natural mothering instincts are similar to the characteristics of shepherding. Women should take this into consideration when evaluating their gifts inventory.

THE PASTOR/SHEPHERD

The spirit-given capacity and desire to serve God by overseeing, training, and caring for the needs of a group of Christians.

The shepherd who leads and feeds: The coach of the "TEAM."

Recognize that the following characteristics are a mixture of the gift of shepherding in any capacity and the gift of shepherding in the capacity of senior pastor. The term "he" is used in a generic sense.

I. CHARACTERISTICS

A. He is usually patient.

B. He is usually willing to spend time in prayer for others.

C. He is usually a "Jack of All and Master of *One*".

D. He is people-centered. He loves them.

E. He is often authoritative in his bearing.

F. He is more a leader than a follower.

G. He is expressive, composed and sensitive.

H. He draws people to himself easily.

I. He has a pleasing personality.

II. BURDENS, DESIRES AND STRENGTHS

A. He has a burden to see others learn and grow.

B. He is protective of those under him.

C. He is burdened to teach the whole Word of God.

D. He usually doesn't like to present the same material more than once.

E. He is willing to study what is necessary to feed his group.

F. He is more relationship oriented than task oriented.

G. He wishes to give direction to those under his care.

H. He desires to look after the spiritual welfare of others.

I. He has a high sense of empathy; is tolerant of people's weaknesses.

J. He is able to resolve problems between people, compromising rather than going to either extreme — a peacemaker and diplomat.

K. He is sensitive to hurt feelings or problems which cause loss of unity.

L. He has a sensitivity to the overall attitude and spirit of the flock.

M. He remembers people's names and faces.

N. He is self-sacrificing when it comes to his flock.
O. He is more concerned with doing for you than you doing for him.
P. He is faithful and devoted to his flock, often becoming a workaholic.
Q. He learns to become an all-purpose person in order to meet needs.

III. SPECIAL NEEDS AND WEAKNESSES

A. He fails to involve other people.
B. He becomes too involved by doing it all himself, becomes too independent.
C. He doesn't make people accountable to the rest of the group.
D. He may become unevangelistic because he already has as many as he can shepherd.
E. He may become overly protective of his flock.
F. He tends to use other people.

IV. HOW HE IS MISUNDERSTOOD BY OTHERS

A. Others think it is his job to do all the work.
B. Others think he should always be available.
C. Others think he knows all the answers.
D. Others think he should be at every social function.
E. Others think he should do all the evangelism.

V. HOW SATAN ATTACKS THIS GIFT

A. Causes discouragement because the load gets heavy.
B. Causes pride because his sheep look up to him.
C. Causes family problems because of too little time and attention.
D. Causes selfishness when "sheep" feed in other pastures.

VI. WHERE TO USE THIS GIFT

A. As a Sunday School teacher.
B. As a Pastor or Assistant Pastor.
C. As a bus captain or bus pastor.
D. As a special ministry leader (youth, children, etc.).
E. As a half-way house, runaway or abuse worker.
F. As a den mother for scout troops.
G. As a dormitory leader in college, orphanage, children's home, etc.

The Mercy Shower

The Greek word is *Ellco*; it means to feel sympathy with or for others. The person with this gift is a comforter and he enters into the grief or happiness of others. He has the ability to show empathy. To show empathy goes beyond sympathy. Sympathy feels *for* others, empathy feels *with* others. The empathizer emotionally goes through what the victim goes through. He ministers to the sick, the poor, the retarded, the prisoners, the blind, the aged, the homely, etc. He's willing to deal with people, and minister to these people — people who have needs that most of us feel very uncomfortable working with.

The MERCY-SHOWER seems to always say the right thing at the right time. He is the one people call first when they hurt because something bad happens or when they feel great because of some good thing happening to them. When there is a death, the mercy-shower is the first to be at the house holding someone's hand or fixing a meal. When there is a promotion on the job or a large amount of money comes in, the mercy-shower runs over and hugs and jumps up and down with the person.

The mercy-shower is generally not found teaching Sunday School or leading a group since his personality is one of soft-spoken love. He's not usually a leader since he would hurt too much if he had to scold someone or have to push to get the job done. People love the mercy-shower because of all the love they receive from him.

Some people think of the mercy-shower as being weak or a compromiser, but he usually has some strong beliefs and principles. It's just that he doesn't like to hurt anyone's feelings, so he doesn't express them very often. People also have a tendency to "use" him since he is so easygoing. When church members visit Aunt Matilda at the nursing home or hospital, they usually spot the mercy-shower since that's where he spends much of his time. The mercy-shower is full of prayer requests at any prayer meeting since he is close to those in the church who are hurting.

When does the mercy-shower best use his gift? In times of sorrow and in times of great joy. The person with this gift often uses it in conjunction with another gift in an area of service, such as deacon, youth worker or hospital visitation. That way he gets the contacts he really wants, those who need his sympathy and to "cry on his shoulder".

The mercy-shower should probably take a counseling course. Since he is sympathetic, he has a tendency not to bring the necessary changes into a person's life to correct the problems that require the counseling. The other alternative is to develop a list of people to whom he can refer people who need counseling or help. That way, he can offer sympathy and understanding and allow someone else to bring about the necessary changes.

For example, if he were to encounter a person who has a problem because of the presence of known sin, it would be good for the mercy-shower to find a prophet who can confront the sin or an exhorter who can give steps to solving the problem. The TEAM concept of counseling is to use the gifted person where his gift will do the most good.

The highest suicide rate among secular occupations amazingly is that of the psychologist — the man with all the answers. The reason is possibly that they attract people with problems. The psychologist is a mercy-shower by nature. He has a sincere desire to help people and he has the ability to sympathize and empathize with people, often putting himself in the other person's shoes. If he takes the other person's problems home with him, it drags him down. Without the Biblical foundation, the counseling often doesn't work, leaving the psychologist under heavy burdens and frustration because of his failure to help people.

The mercy-shower must build some barriers on his feelings. Strong Biblical principles must be established or Satan may use the gift as a stumbling block before the Holy Spirit can use it as a stepping stone.

THE MERCY SHOWER

The Spirit-given capacity and desire to serve God by identifying with and comforting those who are in distress.

The person who understands and comforts his fellow Christian.

I. CHARACTERISTICS

A. He is usually soft-spoken, though talkative.
B. He is outgoing with a low-key inoffensive personality.
C. He finds it very easy to express himself.
D. He appears to always be loving.
E. He is usually good natured, wants people to like him.
F. He talks easily with people and is easy to talk to.
G. He is responsive to people, is a good listener.
H. He is more subjective than objective, decisions are made on feelings more than fact, impulsive.
I. He is peaceable and agreeable, does not overpower others.
J. He does not analyze the details.

II. BURDENS, DESIRES AND STRENGTHS

A. He has a burden to comfort others.
B. He is sympathetic and sensitive.
C. He likes to fellowship with other sympathetic people.
D. His heart goes out to the poor, the aged, the ill, the underprivileged, etc.
E. He is patient, but responds to others' needs quickly.
F. He attracts people who are hurting or rejoicing.
G. He is non-condemning, not a griper (sometimes can be when with other mercy showers).
H. He identifies emotionally and mentally with others.
I. He is patient, sincere, responsive, tolerant.
J. He can become insecure, withdrawn and somewhat remote.
K. He remembers people's names and faces.
L. He is self-sacrificing.
M. He likes to think about things for a while before making decisions.

III. SPECIAL NEEDS AND WEAKNESSES

A. He makes a poor counsellor without additional discipline.
B. He resents others who are not as understanding as he.
C. He is not always logical, but sometimes emotional.
D. He lets others use him.
E. He often has a low self-image.
F. He can be indecisive.
G. He can become a gossiper, especially around other mercy showers.
H. He gets depressed easily.
I. He is controlled by his circumstances.
J. He is pessimistic.

IV. HOW HE IS MISUNDERSTOOD BY OTHERS

A. Others think he is weak.
B. Others think he is a compromiser.
C. Others accuse him of "taking up" for people.
D. Others think he is a "softy".
E. Others think he is too emotional, he cries too easily.

V. HOW SATAN ATTACKS THIS GIFT

A. Causes pride because of his ability to relate to others.
B. Causes disregard for rules and authority.
C. Causes lack of discipline because of strong feeling for those who hurt due to disobedience and sin.
D. Causes him to complain and gripe.

VI. WHERE TO USE THIS GIFT

A. As a hospital, nursing home, shut-in worker.
B. As a funeral coordinator and visitor.
C. As a poverty center worker (if properly disciplined).
D. As an usher or greeter, welcome center worker.
E. As a cassette worker for shut-ins.
F. As a hospitality person.
G. As a telephone center worker.

H. As a member of newcomer team, visiting and telephoning.
I. As a missions worker, committee, correspondence, furlough assistance.
J. As a worker with mentally ill, nursing, blind, deaf, migrant ministry, released offender ministry.

CHAPTER SEVEN

REVIEW QUESTIONS:

1. What type of teacher is the exhorter?

2. What would be a good name for the pastor-teacher? For his followers?

3. When would you want to have the mercy-shower near you?

DISCUSSION QUESTIONS:

1. What do you think is the greatest strength of the exhorter? What would be his greatest weakness?

2. What things should a Sunday School teacher do in exercising his or her gift of pastor-teacher? How can they avoid stepping into the pastor's place of biblical leadership and authority?

3. How has a person with the gift of showing mercy been a blessing in your life?

CHAPTER EIGHT

THE SERVER, THE GIVER, THE ADMINISTRATOR

The Server

The Greek word *Diakonia* means to do service. In Acts 6:1 the word is interpreted *ministration*. Our word deacon comes from the same Greek word. Actually the gift of service is a combination gift — helps and ministering, two expressions of the same gift. The word helps is used in I Corinthians 12:28, and ministering in Romans 12:7. The person with this gift enjoys manual projects. He's not a king. He doesn't even want to be a king. He's happy working behind the scenes. He is a "king-maker".

The SERVER is *not* the person who figures since he can do nothing else in the church, he must have the gift of service. That attitude would belittle the gift and would be an insult to the person who has the gift of serving. There are no menial tasks in God's work. It is possible that more people have this gift than any other. The person with this gift paints the walls, picks up the trash, sorts the hymnals, cleans the baptistry, keeps the nursery, bakes the cakes, cooks the meals, paints the signs, drives the bus, letters the bus and a million and one other necessary tasks in the church. He can always be found late in the evening doing some seemingly small job like fixing the public address speaker that didn't work last Sunday. He usually does not realize that his love for the Lord is showing every time the doors of the church are open, especially if he oiled the hinges last week so they don't squeak any more.

Let's examine *helps* and *ministering* one at a time.

Helps: Many new Christians are highly motivated to serve the Lord; most have to backslide to fit into the average congregation. They are gifted, anxious, motivated, but not yet qualified to do anything but help with the duties of the church. That is why a new Christian should become a HELPER — help in Sunday School or in some other ministry of the church. He should even move around some. As he does, he will start to get a feel for what God has called him to do.

Statistics show that most people who don't get involved in the church's ministry within the first six months will not get involved at all. Yet, six months is hardly enough time to train a new Christian to be a teacher, pastor-teacher or administrator. The best way for a new Christian to get involved and trained while he discovers and develops his dominant gift is in the ministry of HELPS.

Ministering: Many Christians will never graduate from the gift of service because it is their dominant gift. They are always spiritually fulfilled because God gave them this gift and they need not be pushed elsewhere to serve. *Most importantly, the gift of service should never be thought of as a lowly or second-rate ministry.* There was a woman in the Bible that God used as an example of the server. Dorcas (Acts 9:36-42) was a lady who used her talent of sewing in the gift of service. She was faithful in helping the widows of the church where she served. She exercised her gift under the lordship of Christ. Just before Simon Peter arrived for a preaching engagement, Dorcas died. The widows showed Peter the dresses that she had made them. Without her help, they had nothing to wear. Peter was so touched by the scene that he raised Dorcas from the dead.

Simon Peter had a gift too. He had been used mightily by God as a preacher, a healer and even to raise Dorcas from the dead. Surely his gifts were more important to God than Dorcas's little gift of serving. But when Simon Peter died, no one raised him from the dead.

THE SERVER

The Spirit-given capacity and desire to serve God by rendering practical help in both physical and spiritual matters.

The person who meets the practical needs of his fellow Christians and the church.

I. CHARACTERISTICS

A. He is usually ambitious.
B. He doesn't need to be in the public eye to be fulfilled.
C. He enjoys manual projects.
D. He is often involved in a variety of activities and volunteers for many different jobs.
E. He is loyal, sincere, tolerant, faithful and devoted.
F. He is usually easy going, likable, congenial, inoffensive.
G. He usually wants people to like him.
H. He listens to others without being critical.
I. He is usually inhibited publicly, not usually expressive.
J. He is not dominating — more a follower than a leader.
K. He is usually good with mechanical work.

II. BURDENS, DESIRES AND STRENGTHS

A. He is burdened with others' needs, quickly responds to the needs.
B. He is impressed with the need to respond when exhorted to serve.
C. He is usually unable to say, "NO".
D. He will very seldom step in as a leader.
E. He likes to meet immediate needs.
F. He likes to have a good leader he can support.
G. He enjoys doing mechanical or menial jobs in the church.
H. He often has high sense of empathy.
I. He is usually very patient.
J. He avoids drawing attention to himself.
K. He is often considered a workaholic.

III. SPECIAL NEEDS AND WEAKNESSES

A. He may emphasize practical needs over spiritual needs.
B. He is not as concerned about the completed task as he is about the immediate service; has a tendency not to follow through.
C. He may under-emphasize verbal witnessing.
D. He may jump to meet needs in the church or in other homes before those of his own family.
E. He often has a low self-esteem.
F. He needs to know that his efforts are appreciated.
G. He will take his own time, usually working slowly and deliberately
H. He does not stand out in a crowd.
 I. He likes for a task to challenge him.
 J. He will attach himself to someone who is doing exciting things and will allow that excitement to spill over on himself.
K. He is controlled more by circumstances than principles.
L. He is only satisfied when he has done more for you than you have done for him.
M. He avoids long term responsibilities.
N. He is a master of decisive indecision.
O. He reads directions when all else fails.

IV. HOW HE IS MISUNDERSTOOD BY OTHERS

A. Others think he is pushy, doing things without asking leaders.
B. Others think he excludes them.
C. Others think he is impatient and jumps in too fast.
D. Others accuse him of interfering with the Spirit's work.
E. Others think he neglects spiritual needs.

V. HOW SATAN ATTACKS THIS GIFT

A. Causes pride because of work he has done.
B. Causes feeling of insignificance.
C. Causes lack of burden for people.
D. Causes lack of concern for spiritual growth.
E. Causes lack of quality workmanship due to lack of knowledge or skills.

VI. WHERE TO USE THIS GIFT

A. As person in charge of maintenance and grounds.
B. As a baptismal helper.
C. As a nursery, kitchen or choir helper.
D. As an office worker, errand runner.
E. As an audio-video worker.
F. As a record keeper.
G. As a librarian in church library or cassette ministry.
H. As a greeter or an usher.
I. As an instrumentalist or choir member in music department.
J. As a stage hand in drama productions.
K. As a photographer.
L. As a helper in special ministries such as migrants, deaf, etc.
M. As a hospitality worker for newcomers or visitors.

The Giver

The Greek word *Metadidomi* means to give over, to share, to give to, to impart. The important thing here is not to spiritualize and explain away this gift. Some say that this gift refers to giving of yourself and your time, that it doesn't really mean giving your money. On the contrary, the GIVER honestly feels that the best way he can give of himself is to give of his material gain for the work of God. He feels that since God gave him the ability to make money, he should use it to give back to God and His work. Everyone should tithe, but the giver goes far beyond the tithe.

The Scriptures point out giving as one of the gifts in Romans 12. The giver is encouraged to give "in simplicity" (Romans 12:8). Most Christians with the gift of giving do so without fanfare and public recognition. In fact, the giver usually does not wish for people to know who he is nor how much is given.

The attitude of the giver is that tithing is the outward evidence of an inward commitment. Tithing is not giving 10 percent, it's receiving 90 percent. It is a commandment for all Christians. The gift of giving starts where tithing ends off.

The giver would look with disapproval on the person who gives with the wrong motive — giving to get (trying to intimidate God into returning the monetary gift). He would not encourage giving grocery money, but would agree with giving the money that was saved toward a new TV. His motive for giving is always to further the work of God and not to "show off" though some might think otherwise of him.

In Acts 4:34-5:10, there is a significant description of people who had unusual opportunities to give. In the early church, Christian landowners often sold their land and other possessions and gave the proceeds to the church in order to care for those who were in need. One of those men was Barnabas. He sold his land and laid the money at the Apostles' feet (Acts 4:36-37). But Ananias and Sapphira sold their land and schemed to give only part of the money to the Lord's work. They lied and tried to deceive the apostles (Acts 5:1-10). It is interesting to compare the attitudes and the rewards those attitudes received. Barnabas eventually accompanied the Apostle Paul in much of his ministry. Ananias and Sapphira were killed by God as a result of their treachery.

The proper attitude about the gift of giving is probably best illustrated by the story of the Honorable Alpheus Hardy, who used money to support missionaries and educate ministers. His monetary support helped lay the foundations for Christianity in Japan.

During college, Hardy's health broke and he discovered he could not become a minister. "My distress was so great I threw myself flat on the floor," he said of one morning's depression. "I cannot be God's minister kept rolling in my mind. It was the voiceless cry of my soul."

During that ordeal God revealed to Hardy that he could serve God with similar devotion in business. To make money for God might be his special calling and gift. The answer was so clear and joyous he exclaimed aloud, "O God, I can be Thy minister." Making money and giving it to God became his ministry.

Another example of how a man's gift of giving can be so greatly used is Dr. Oswald J. Smith, writer of the song "Then Jesus Came". His desire was to become a missionary. Instead, God placed him in the pastorate and used him to send missionaries and money for missions all over the world. He is recognized as one of the greatest missionary statesmen of recent history.

There must be a distinction made between the gift of giving and the grace of giving. First, realize that tithing and giving are responsibilities of every Christian. The tithe is the first fruits of our increase. It is God's and we should give it to Him immediately. Luke 6:38 is for every Christian, not just those with the gift of giving. That is the grace of giving — giving from a heart of love, allowing God to furnish the returns when we have given from a desire to help others and further His work.

An evangelist visited a college campus where I was attending for a week of meetings. His inspiring messages on giving inspired personal testimonies from students who gave and received throughout the week. Many caught the spirit and gave and gave. The problem, though, didn't surface until several weeks later when the students' bills came due. They couldn't pay their bills; they had given the money away. What went wrong? After all, the Scripture does say to give and you will receive.

First of all, the evangelist was not aware of the gift of giving. He failed to tell us (or was unaware) that all the people in the many overwhelming testimonies had the gift of giving. When it comes to giving and receiving, there are principles which apply only to those with the gift of giving (such as the ability to give beyond their means).

Secondly, the students did not have their hearts in the right place. They were not giving to help God as much as to help themselves. *Motive* is the key to giving and receiving. The proper motive is giving to receive in order to give again. These young people were giving to receive so they would have more at the end.

Many Christians, in sheer desperation, have given all they had trying to bale themselves out of a jam, only to see their efforts fail. You can't *give* yourself out of a financial jam nor can you *give* your way to prosperity with that end as a motive.

Four guidelines must be observed by the giver:
1. Do not love riches.
2. Give for the right reason.
3. Make giving your reason for gaining wealth.
4. Keep your spiritual life a constant walk with God.

THE GIVER

The Spirit-given capacity and desire to serve God by giving of his material resources, far beyond the tithe, to further the work of God.

The person who meets the financial need of his fellow Christians and church members.

I. CHARACTERISTICS

A. He is usually well organized.
B. He keeps to himself.
C. He doesn't like his giving to be publicized.
D. He usually has the ability to make money as well, *but not always*.
E. He has an accurate self-image.
F. He is more likely to be lighthearted than depressed.
G. He is particularly interested in helping people.
H. He wants people to like him.
I. He is conscientious and self-disciplined.

II. BURDENS, DESIRES AND STRENGTHS

A. He is sensitive to the financial and material needs of others.
B. He is alert to needs others might overlook.
C. He is always ready to give.
D. He wants his gift to be of high quality.
E. He has the ability to make quick decisions concerning finances.
F. He wants to know his gift is being used properly.
G. He usually has a burden for missions.
H. He is not the first to give to a project, but will wait for the project to prove itself.
I. He is sympathetic.

III. SPECIAL NEEDS AND WEAKNESSES

A. He may measure others' spirituality by the amount of their giving.
B. He judges others' success by the amount of their material assets.

C. He thinks God has called everyone to give as he does, and cannot understand why they ignore the calling.
D. He usually gives to projects, but not to individuals.

IV. HOW HE IS MISUNDERSTOOD BY OTHERS

A. Others think he is trying to control them with his money.
B. Others think he condemns them because they don't give as he does.
C. Others think he condemns them because they don't have as much as he does.
D. Others are sometimes jealous of him.
E. Others think he is materialistic because of his emphasis on money.
F. Others think he tries to buy a position in the church.

V. HOW SATAN ATTACKS THIS GIFT

A. Causes pride because of the amount of his gift.
B. Causes blindness to spiritual needs and qualities.
C. Causes blindness to other areas of service.
D. Causes discontent when decisions are made contrary to where his interests are or where he has given.
E. Causes critical attitude of those unable to give.
F. Causes wrong motives for giving or serving Christ.
G. Causes him to mistake a burden for giving to missions as a call to the mission field ministry.

VI. WHERE TO USE THIS GIFT

A. Anywhere large *or* small amounts of money are needed.
B. As a member of finance or budget committee.
C. As a member of missions committee, building committee.
D. As a trustee.
E. As a member of school board or commission.
F. As a part of poverty, rescue mission, migrant mission committee member.
G. As a sponsor to underwrite special projects, radio, TV ministries.
H. To meet needs of an individual apart from programs.

The Administrator

A *Kubernesis* (in the Greek) was a steersman for a ship. He had the responsibility of bringing a ship into the harbor — through the rocks and shoals under all types of pressures.

Charles Swindoll says, "A *Kubernesis* was an expert in the midst of a storm," a good definition for the gift of administration. Leading, ruling, organizing, governing, and administering are words that come from different translations of the Scriptures of the same Greek word.

The ADMINISTRATOR is a "take charge" person who jumps in and starts giving orders when no one is in charge (sometimes when someone else is in charge). He puts a plan on paper and starts delegating responsibility. The committee or group reports back to him and he works the whole scheme of the program together.

If there is a program or event to take place, he almost instantly has a plan to carry it out. When followed, the plan usually makes it more effective.

There are actually two leadership styles. One organizes things, events or programs. The other organizes people and emphasizes personal relationships and leadership responsibilities.

Perhaps the administrator is chairman of the board or the Deacons. In fact, without such a chairman, the board will not function at its best. Some people think he takes too much on himself. Sometimes he has to watch that he doesn't overstep his authority and expect the pastor or others in leadership to follow him. On the surface he is extremely organized. If he organizes things or events, he will usually organize details and have people carry them out. If he is prone to organize people, he is not a detail person, but relies on others to take care of the little things.

He does not often admit to mistakes. He usually does not take time to explain to those under him why he is doing things; he just expects the job to get done. His patience may wear thin when plans are not carried through as he laid them out.

When things in the church become fragmented, he can harmonize the whole program if given a chance. As soon as a task is completed, he is already working on the next event and starts giving the directions before others even catch a breath. He leads by saying, "Come on, keep up with me and we'll set the world on fire."

Close observation reveals that most pastors of large churches have this gift. Their ability to lead is a major factor causing the churches to become large.

But what about the small church where most of us are? Every position in your church that requires leadership is a potential area to practice this gift. The chairman of the deacons, trustees or another committee, the Sunday School Superintendent — all these areas should have people in them who have leadership ability.

It would be much wiser and more effective if churches would place people who have the gift of administration in positions of leadership. It would work better than using a rotation basis in positions such as deacon chairman or trustee chairman. It may sound good that the rotation system keeps one person from becoming a dictator or getting too much control. However, such a system often causes a gap in progress if someone without the gift of administration is in leadership for a year or more.

The answer is to retain men who are leaders in leadership positions, keeping them in check with the Scriptures and providing adequate and ongoing training. They need to learn the four aces of leadership in I Corinthians 11:1 (an easy way to remember it — the four ones), "Be ye followers of me, even as I also *am of Christ.*" When one of God's men gets a large following, the question is always asked: "Yeah, but are they following God or the man?" They can clearly see that many of these people would not be following God if the man wasn't present. The point is though, God has always had His men. Would the Israelites have left Egypt if they hadn't had Moses, or would they have conquered the Promised Land without Joshua? God could have chosen a number of ways to lead His people, but He chose the same method for leading as He did for the rest of His work here on earth — MEN. Throughout history God has always had His men for leading: Saul, David, Gideon, Nehemiah, Solomon and men like Paul. Some were good and some bad.

Have you ever read I and II Chronicles? It can be boring and confusing with all the genealogies and "begats", but one thing is certain. You will find that all through Israel's history, when there was Godly leadership, Israel prospered and when there was poor leadership, there was failure.

Even since Bible times, God's leaders are recognized; men like Martin Luther, John Calvin, John Knox, Charles Finney, John Wesley, George Mueller, Dwight L. Moody and John R. Rice. But from the very beginning, *in the minds of the people*, God's great leaders always stopped with the previous generation. Why is it that a man must be dead before we are willing to follow him, when God has His men for every generation, including ours?

THE ADMINISTRATOR

The Spirit-given capacity and desire to serve God by organizing, administering, promoting and leading the various affairs of the church. The man who leads the church and its ministries.

I. CHARACTERISTICS

A. He is a man with a dream.
B. He is goal oriented.
C. He is well-disciplined.
D. He usually works best under heavy pressure.
E. He is not a procrastinator.
F. He is often a good motivator.
G. He is serious minded, highly motivated, intense.
H. He has an accurate self-image.
I. He is more interested in the welfare of the group than his own desires.
J. He is a perfectionist. He wants what he is involved in done well.
K. He loves drafts, charts and lists.
L. He wants things done *his* way *now*.
M. He is a workaholic.
N. He keeps his emotions hidden.
O. He is bored with the trivial.
P. He is dominant, not passive.
Q. He likes to be center-stage with people looking at him.

II. BURDENS, DESIRES AND STRENGTHS

A. He dreams big dreams for God.
B. He has a burden to move on to a new task as soon as he has completed one, usually having already planned it.
C. He delegates wherever possible, but knows where he can't.
D. He can't bear defeat. He wants to win.
E. He can harmonize the various affairs of the church.
F. He is willing to attempt impossible tasks.
G. He is capable of making quick decisions and sticking to them.
H. He will assume leadership when there is no leadership in the group.

I. He is skilled in planning.

J. He makes decisions logically, strictly on facts, not feelings.

K. He is more composed than nervous.

L. He follows many sports events. He is competitive by nature.

M. He likes tasks that challenge him.

N. He is enthusiastic, gets people excited.

O. He plans ahead and works on a schedule.

P. He demonstrates competence.

Q. He sees the whole picture quickly.

III. SPECIAL NEEDS AND WEAKNESSES

A. He appears on the outside to be organized, but usually isn't.

B. He looks at the overall picture and may miss the smaller details.

C. He may make decisions based on logic rather than Scripture.

D. He doesn't like to admit to making a mistake or to weaknesses.

E. He may be insensitive to "little" people.

F. He is often hard to please. His standards are too high. He is not tolerant of mistakes.

G. He is not good at remembering names.

H. He may not be gracious when hurried or busy.

I. He will manipulate others into doing what he wants done. He uses people.

IV. HOW HE IS MISUNDERSTOOD BY OTHERS

A. Others think he is cold.

B. Others think he is pushy.

C. Others think he is using them because of his lack of explanation.

D. Others think he is not concerned with people.

E. Others think he doesn't have time for others.

F. Others think he is selfish, trying to be a big shot.

G. Others think he is lazy if he administrates without getting involved himself.

H. Others think he is bossy and impatient.

I. Others think he is too independent.

V. HOW SATAN ATTACKS THIS GIFT

A. Causes pride because of leadership role.
B. Causes selfishness because of success, not sharing glory with those under him.
C. Causes blame-shifting when things go wrong.
D. Causes discouragement and frustration when goals aren't met or things go too slow.
E. Causes anger and mistreatment of those who disagree with plans, goals and methods.
F. Causes wrong motives.
G. Causes lack of concern for people or their needs.
H. Causes lack of spiritual growth and qualities.

VI. WHERE TO USE THIS GIFT

A. As the leader of each project, ministry or program.
B. As chairman of any committee or board.
C. As church planner or coordinator.
D. As pastor or assistant pastor, business manager.
E. As an office manager or department head for large staffs.
F. As a Sunday School superintendent, deacon chairman.
G. As the chairman of building or fundraising projects.
H. As the nursery coordinator.
 I. As a leader of men's fellowship.
 J. As the head of the library.
K. As a camp director, bus ministry head.
L. As head of Vacation Bible School.
M. As a women's missionary circle or fellowship leader.
N. As the church moderator.

Now What?

Did you recognize anyone in these last three chapters? If you read carefully, you probably found a description of yourself and probably recognized your spiritual gift whether or not you have taken and graded the Gifts Profile (see Chapter Twelve). You probably also saw someone in your church with whom you previously have had misunderstanding and problems. Other gifts will have certain characteristics which are completely opposite from the characteristic of your gift. In light of this, you need to go back through these last three chapters and really analyze what you have read. As you do so, take a pencil and write at the top of the page the name of a person who fits the description in the outline. (No one will be 100%, but all fit into a generalized category.) After you have done that, ask yourself if you have misjudged the motives and lifestyle of that person because of some of the characteristics which are opposite of those of your own gift.

When we understand our gifts, we can understand, accept and feel comfortable with ourselves. It is just as important that we understand others in the body of Christ who have gifts differing from our own. The secret of unity and understanding in the local body may rest in understanding gift characteristics. As a result, we will love and accept people *because of* rather than *in spite of* those characteristics.

Everyone is different because of the particular spiritual gift he possesses. We do not have to remake everyone to fit into our mold. We must accept others and amplify their strengths while we overlook their weaknesses. We also must work to amplify our own strengths while we work prayerfully and diligently to overcome our own weaknesses. (By the way, this is also true within the family. It is easier to understand our mates and other family members when we understand their spiritual gifts and the characteristics of those gifts.)

CHAPTER EIGHT

REVIEW QUESTIONS:

1. If the server is not a king, what is he? Why?

2. What does a giver usually give to the church and ministry?

3. What gift is recommended for leadership roles in the ministry?

DISCUSSION QUESTIONS:

1. How important is the person with the gift of serving? Why?

2. Why do you think that givers often do not want people to know how often, how much or when they give?

3. What kind of obstacles can the person with the gift of administration have with other people in the church? How can their reactions hinder the work of God?

SECTION THREE

EQUIPPING THE TEAM

INTRODUCTION

Sooner or later, almost everyone has a craving for pizza. When that happens, nothing else will satisfy the appetite but pizza. A person will not go to the ice cream parlor or the hamburger haven to take care of that craving. Those places don't meet the need of the hour — pizza. The finest steak dinner in an exclusive restaurant or the largest and finest lobster will not do the job. They simply do not satisfy the need for pizza. Only the pizza parlor will be able to meet the need for pizza.

Likewise only the gifted people in the church can be the vehicle God uses to meet the needs of a lost and dying generation. *People will support the church that meets the needs in their lives, or touches the lives and needs of their loved ones.* Not only must the church meet the need, but it must also meet the need when it occurs. The church which can meet the need of a person when it occurs will have the best chance of reaching and keeping any person for Christ.

There are two kinds of needs: felt needs and real needs. Sometimes the felt needs are not real needs and the real needs are sometimes not felt by a person. The church must meet those needs, sometimes pointing out the real need in the person's life so that it becomes a felt need. Sometimes the felt need must be met first in order to discover the real need. In other words, the church must meet both felt and real needs.

How can that best be done? By using the "TEAM Gifts" in the lives of the members to reach out to the needs of the lost in the community. For every need in the life of the lost person, there is a gift that helps reach that person for Christ. When the lost receive Christ, there are still needs which must be met. Again, the TEAM comes to the rescue, meeting those needs through the spiritual gifts God gave for that purpose.

What I really wish to discuss here is how the balanced church meets all the needs that exist in the body. But before I do that, I must first address the *purpose* of the church. For only a church that is effectively fulfilling its God-given purpose can effectively minister to the needs of its community and membership.

The Purpose Of The Church

The church's Great Commission is found in Matthew 28:19-20, "Go ye therefore, and teach all nations, baptizing them in the name of the

Father, and of the Son, and of the Holy Ghost: teaching them to observe all things whatsoever I have commanded you: and, lo, I am with you alway, even unto the end of the world."

Take note that the word "teach" is in the Great Commission twice. Going back to the original language you'll find the first "teach", *matheteuo* (Greek), in verse 19. "Teach all nations" does not mean teach as we think of teaching. That word literally means, "to make disciples". Making disciples of someone in Bible times was not what we consider making disciples today. We seem to think that when a person gets saved he becomes a Christian. When he later devotes his life to the Lord and really starts serving God, then we call him a disciple.

Believers were never called Christians until Antioch, when the believers began imitating Christ. They acted so much like Christ that the people could see Christ in them. So the people started to call them "Christones" or Christians. We have it backwards. We think that when a person gets saved, he becomes a Christian. Actually at the time of the new birth, the person becomes a disciple. When he matures and starts acting like Christ, that's when he becomes a Christian.

In verse 20, the word "teaching" is another Greek word, *didasko*, meaning "to teach". Therefore, if we are to teach all nations and to teach them to observe *all things*, that gives us a two-part commission. The commission is not simply to go out and present the gospel to people. It is to present the gospel to people and train them. It is a two-part commission — to *reach* and *teach*.

The great commission was given to the church. It was given to you and me as a cooperating part of a local body. It is to be fulfilled by a group of Christians working together with one common goal: to *reach* and *teach* the world. (At the same time, we are supportive of people who are reaching and teaching to keep all the needs in the church met so we can have a unit that can continue *reaching* and *teaching*.

The Purpose Of The Bible

Since we understand that the purpose for the church is to *reach* and to *teach*, we also must understand that the *Bible* was also given to us for the same purpose. *Reaching* and *teaching* simply means getting a man converted, training him,teaching him, instructing him and helping him mature into the image of Christ.

II Timothy 3:15-17 says "And that from a child thou hast known the Holy Scriptures, which are able to make thee wise unto salvation through faith which is in Christ Jesus. All Scripture is given by inspiration of God, and is profitable for doctrine, for reproof, for correction, for instruction in righteousness: that the man of God may be perfect, throughly furnished unto all good works."

This passage gives us the full purpose of the Bible. Verse 15 says the Scriptures are "able to make thee wise unto salvation" (that's reaching). Verses 16 and 17 tell us how to train a Christian. The Scriptures are to be used for doctrine (what to believe), reproof (what not to do, pointing out sin), correction (how to change) and instruction in righteousness (how to live right). In other words, the Bible is for *reaching* a lost man, then *teaching* him into full maturity.

Many churches would say, "We're doing that, but something is still wrong. We're winning them, but they're not staying around. They're going out the back door as fast as others come in the front door. Also, we can't seem to get people involved."

I suggest that many of these churches are having problems because they are not meeting the needs of their people. That is where spiritual gifts come in — equipping the saints for service so that needs can be met in other people's lives.

CHAPTER NINE

THE TEAM VERSUS THE LOST

A number of years ago, I started teaching a Sunday School class. I had never taught before, nor had I had any teacher training. However, I did realize that if I was going to be successful, not only was there certain material that needed to be taught, but I had to meet definite needs in the lives of my students as well.

I was teaching young adults. However, my classes didn't always go as I had planned them. I'd bomb out now and then. Being an analytical person, I always asked the question, "Why didn't it work?"

Every week I was off to the Christian Book Store to buy a new book. After much study I realized the books reinforced the fact that if I was going to minister and teach people I had to meet certain needs in their lives. Not just one or two, but several needs, if I was to be effective in ministering to the *whole* person. In fact, I came up with a list of eleven needs.

Later, when I studied the subject of spiritual gifts, I was amazed as God pointed out to me the correlation between these needs and the spiritual gifts. The characteristics of each gift met a need that was evident. The more I studied, the more I could see how they dove-tailed together perfectly. There were the needs of the people on one side that had to be met, and the gifts with characteristics that ministered to the needs on the other.

The chart titled "The Team Versus the Lost" is the result of that study. The left side lists the needs that the church must meet in the life of a believer if he is to mature as a Christian.

The other side of the chart is the gift that predominantly ministers to that particular need.

You will notice the progression of the chart leads from the first need of getting a person saved (reaching) and takes him to being a complete, mature Christian (teaching). This chart is built assuming the purpose of the church, as laid out in the previous introduction, is to *reach* and *teach*. The job of the church (TEAM) is to reach the world (LOST) with the gospel, getting each person saved, and leading him to becoming a mature Christian.

MAN NEEDS

1 Salvation

2 the EVANGELISTS

3 Awareness of Sin

4 the PROPHETS

5 Doctrine

6 the TEACHERS

7 To Know How

8 the EXHORTERS

9 Shepherding

10 the PASTOR/SHEPHERD

11 Comforting

12 the MERCY SHOWERS

13 A Helping Hand

14 the SERVERS

15 Financial Aid

16 the GIVERS

17 Leadership

18 the ADMINISTRATORS

19 Fellowship

20 the ENTIRE BODY

21 to Serve His Fellow Man

22 A Mature Christian

23 the "TEAM"

24 "LASTING GROWTH"

Let's look at the needs one at a time and see how God has equipped the church to minister to it. (The numbering system will help you follow the chart.)

Number (1): Man's first need is *salvation*. Romans 3:23 says, "For all have sinned, and come short of the glory of God."

Who is the TEAM member who meets this need in his life? The (2) *evangelist*. This is not to say the evangelist is the only person in a church to lead people to a saving knowledge of Jesus Christ. But if you took a poll, you would see that he is the person who will probably reach eighty or ninety percent of them. He is a salesman for Christ. He is aggressive and confrontational.

What is meant by a confrontational evangelist (called a soul-winner by some)? He is the type of person who is always trying to motivate others to reach out to lost people. He's also the person who gives the testimony, "I went on a trip and I sat down next to a guy who wasn't saved." He ends the story by saying, "As the plane touched down, the gentleman beside me bowed his head and accepted Christ as his Saviour." He gets on an elevator with a "sinner" on the sixth floor and he gets off on the twelfth floor with a "saint". Again, I need to stress that he's not the only person to lead a person to Christ, but we must accept the fact that a gifted evangelist gets most of the decisions whether he was the one who really influences them for Christ or not.

Number (3) is man's need to be *made aware of sin*. The person who meets this need in his life is a (4) *prophet*. He's the type of person who can see what's wrong in people's lives. He can see what's wrong in a church, although his ability to see everything that is right is limited. His ministry is preaching, and usually that of pointing out sin. He preaches for conviction, and he does what we think of as real preaching. We think of a preacher as somebody who gets excited, steps on toes, and preaches for conviction. His preaching really stirs your heart. He is the Hellfire/brimstone preacher.

Number (5) is that he needs to *know the principles for right living*, in other words, *what is right*. The person who meets this need in his life is the (6) *teacher*. *Didasko* is the Greek word which means to teach: to communicate knowledge, to relay facts, or to make known.

Number (7) is the need to *know "how"*. The person who meets that need in his life is the (8) *exhorter*. He is the one who spends much time teaching people how to do things. He also is a motivator of people, exciting them about getting more done.

Number (9) is the need to *be cared for like a sheep*. Who meets that need in his life? The (10) *pastor-teacher*. He has the shepherd approach to leadership. He is burdened to teach the Word of God and to care for the people around him. He is protective and shelters them.

Number (11) is the need to *be comforted*. Who would meet that need? The (12) *mercy shower*. He is the soft-spoken, but outgoing person who seems to always know what to say when we hurt.

Let's say a tragedy was to happen in your life. Who would be the first person that you would call? Most would call someone with the gift of showing mercy. People with the gift of showing mercy attract people who are hurting. They also attract people who are having good times, people in times of joy

Number (13) is that man needs *a helping hand*. In order to keep a church from falling down, people who are willing to do the maintenance and take care of the building are needed. The (14) *server* is the person that meets that need because the server is the person who is very content doing the physical labor around the church. This is a definite ministry that we need to promote today. It's a gift that God has given to many people in all churches.

Number (15) is the need for *financial aid*. Finances are needed to support the ministries and the missions in the church. The person who meets this need is the (16) *giver*. The giver is very mission minded and it's not unusual to see a church that has several givers in it to be supporting many mission projects. This is another ministry that's drastically needed today, and we should never belittle people who have this gift.

I'm thankful that as I went through Bible School there were people that had the gift of giving and helped us with financial needs. We probably would never have been able to make it without their help.

At this point, I need to point out something of importance. Giving and serving are two gifts we really need an extra emphasis on today, because we've allowed government to take over in these areas. We give to churches to add a wing on the church, but when it comes to giving to a Christian, the individual, we don't do that anymore. We're having government take over to make up for the Christians' failure to do what is right.

When a person in the church has problems, the Christians usually say something like, "Can you borrow the money some place to get straightened out?" or "Surely there is some type of a welfare program that'll help," or "You can have the money if you sign a note and pay it back monthly with interest." The point I am trying to get across is, we're telling people to go some place else. But God says, in Romans 12:13, that we Christians are to meet those needs in people's lives. He says, "distributing to the necessity of the saints" — and the saints are the Christians — "given to hospitality". It's our job to take care of and to meet the needs of those people in the Body and not pawn them off on government. It was never government's job to start with (read Acts chapter 6). Government picked up on it simply because the Christians were failing by not ministering the gift that God had given them. I believe these two gifts, giving and serving, are the most prevalent gifts in most of our churches.

Number (17): Man is a follower. In order to reach a goal, eighty-four percent of the people need a total program planned for them with constant supervision. If the program is laid out, fourteen percent of the people have the ability to meet that goal with little supervision. Only two percent of the people have the ability to create a dream and carry it through to completion by themselves. These latter people are the (18) *administrators.* They are the leaders. Man needs leadership.

Number (19) is the need for *fellowship.* Who meets this need? The (20) *entire body* does. All the administrators, the servers, the givers, the exhorters, the prophets, the teachers, the evangelists, the mercy showers and the pastor-teachers. All these people combined together, the entire body, meet the fellowship need in a person's life. By the way, polls have shown that most people who start attending a certain church, do so for the fellowship they enjoy. We go to church to be with our friends. In a big church, a stranger has the tendency not to meet people and mix with people. It is hard to find new friends and a group with whom to fellowship. It is more difficult to meet the need of fellowship in a larger church, but it can and must be done.

Number (21) in the center and sideways on the chart is man's need to *serve his fellow man.* This is what I call the *catalyst need.* That's why it is between the needs and the gifts. It ties together the whole concept of spiritual gifts meeting needs. *Man needs to serve his fellow man.* It's a need put in the hearts of all men by God. It's people wrapping their lives up in the lives of others.

It doesn't have to be just Christians. Anywhere that people are willing to wrap their lives up in the lives of other people, you'll see happier, more contented, and less troubled people — simply because they are meeting a God-given need. As Christians, we need to serve our fellow man by the ministering of our spiritual gifts.

A recent television commercial says, "People helping people, that's what life is all about." That *is* what life's all about. The most miserable people I know are selfish, concerned only with themselves and their own welfare. They're miserable and they make everyone around them just as miserable as they are.

Let's add (as if this were a math problem) the left side of the chart. What do we get? (22) *A mature Christian.* After you have met all these needs in a man's life, he becomes a mature Christian. Of course, if you don't meet all the needs in his life, he won't become quite as mature. For every need we don't meet, he will be that much less mature. But, the closer we come to meeting all the needs, the more mature the individual will become.

Tragically though, many churches miss one, two, three, or even all of the top four needs. To keep from making this mistake, we need to understand the *biblical procedure* for training Christians.

II Timothy 3:16 states, "All Scripture is given by inspiration of God, and is profitable" for four things: "for doctrine, for reproof, for correction, for instruction in righteousness." We quote this Scripture very often to support the fact that we have an inerrant Bible. But, let's look one step further and see what is the *biblical procedure* for training Christians. The procedure is first: doctrine, second: reproof, third: correction and fourth: instruction. I don't think it is any accident these four items appear in your Bible in this order.

Doctrine is the norms and standards of the Scriptures. It teaches the standards by which we must govern our lives and our ministries. Doctrine is not the process of teaching, but the product of teaching. The second step is *reproof.* To reprove, you show what is wrong. Next is *correction.* To correct, you show what is right. *Instruction* is simply "how to", or practical application.

Notice the relationship. First, the ministry of the *prophet* is simply pointing out *what is wrong,* and the ministry of the *teacher* is simply pointing out *what is right.* The ministry of the *exhorter* is simply telling *how to* do it.

We have a tendency to skip some of these people, and usually the person we like to skip is the prophet. After all, who wants a preacher stepping on our toes. The prophet makes us uncomfortable. In turn, we keep those who make us uncomfortable out of our lives.

Or, many churches lack a gifted teacher, and a sound doctrinal foundation for their ministry. The person who is doctrine oriented is usually fact oriented rather than oriented to the practical application. But a good teacher, teaching theology, doctrine and prophecy week in and week out without giving practical application will have a frustrated congregation.

One of the most evident things lacking in meeting people's needs is simple, practical, "how to" teaching. For instance, consider the man that says, "I know I'm a rotten father, and I know I do things wrong, but I'm tired of people telling me what I'm doing wrong. I want somebody to show me *how to* become a better father."

On the other hand, you can't teach a man how to be a better father if you haven't first convicted him that he needs to be a better father. Without conviction, practical teaching will go in one ear and out the other. At the same time, the practical teacher can't be effective if his teaching is not based on the sound doctrine, proper theology, which comes about by the teacher.

Sometimes we have teachers that can do both. Besides teaching, they have the gifts of prophecy and exhortation. But it usually works like this: the prophet will get him stirred up, or convicted; and the practical teacher comes in and gives him the "how to", enabling him to change his life. The teacher gives him the doctrinal teaching and biblical facts that will prevent him from falling into sin again. This type of situation further emphasizes the balance and cooperation within the body as described in the Bible when it deals with spiritual gifts.

I want you to understand I am not talking about exclusiveness. Example: A man comes into your church for help and the secretary says, "Are you saved?" He says, "No." So she says, "In that case, first, you need to go to the end of the hall and see Rev. Evangelist, so he can get you saved. Then you need to go across the hall and see Mr. Prophet so he can tell you what's wrong. Then come back up the hall to see Dr. Teacher so he can show you what's right, then go upstairs and let Counselor Exhorter show you how to solve your problems."

No, I'm not talking about such exclusiveness, but I am talking about people who will excel in these different areas of the ministry because of the gift God has given them. There will be much overlap in all the areas.

When the right side of the chart is added together, it totals The TEAM.

Number (23) — The TEAM is a group of active people indwelled and empowered by the Holy Spirit. No doubt about it, this is the most powerful force on this earth, and for years we have let this force lay mostly dormant. We have the most powerful force on earth, yet by doing nothing with it, we're letting the world and humanism take over our schools, government, etc. As said by Edmund Burke, "All it takes for evil to triumph is for good men to do nothing."

Number (24): This is the real bottom line — Lasting Growth.

For lasting growth, the church has to meet ALL these needs in the members' lives. When you miss some of these needs, it leaves people incomplete and they subconsciously look to fulfill the missing needs. In many cases, they're not even aware that the needs exist. All they know is there's an emptiness in their lives, and they just move on. They look for another church that can meet their needs. Sometimes after moving through several churches, they drop out completely, thinking that no church can meet their needs. Of course, very few churches can minister effectively to all these needs. But, the more that are met the more effective the church will be in lasting growth.

Balance — The Ultimate

Some churches are strong on outreach. They're getting people saved. But at the same time people are going out the back door, because they don't have a good support program to back up their evangelism. Some have good teaching ministries, but don't evangelize. The whole idea is balance. The balanced church is a growing and effective church.

The Analogy of the Body

In all three places where Paul writes on spiritual gifts (Romans 12, I Corinthians 12 and Ephesians 4), he uses a three way analogy of the human body, the body of Christ and spiritual gifts. The church is compared to the human body. The parts of the body are compared to the members of the church with the various spiritual gifts. I Corinthians 12 says, "For as the body is one, and hath many members, and all the members of that one body, being many, are one body: so also is Christ

. . .For the body is not one member, but many. If the foot shall say, because I am not the hand, I am not of the body; is it therefore not of the body?. . .If the whole body were an eye, where were the hearing? If the whole were hearing, where were the smelling? But now hath God set the members every one of them in the body as it hath pleased Him...And the eye cannot say unto the hand, I have no need of thee: nor again the head to the feet, I have no need of thee. Nay, much more those members of the body, which seem to be more feeble are necessary."

Paul's analogy of the human body is an excellent example to explain this principle. For we can take the human body and chop off a hand —as a matter of fact you can chop off the whole arm — you can chop off both arms, both legs, both ears, chop off the nose, punch out the eyes, pull out the hair, knock out the teeth, and although the body is seriously handicapped, it does not cease to function; it just doesn't function efficiently.

The question is, *when does the body function most efficiently?* When it is all there; when every member is there and doing what it is suppose to do. When the hands are being hands, the feet are being feet, the ears are being ears, and they are all working together for one common goal.

To develop this effective TEAM we must have all the gifts operating in one local church, thus meeting the needs of all the people in that church or community. We complement each other and we meet the needs of each other; therefore, we make an effective TEAM.

The Little Toe Principle

You might say, "I know that I'm part of the body, but I'm just the little toe. I'm really not needed. I don't have much part in the body, and I'm not effective at all."

I once knew a man who had his little toe cut off in an accident. If you're the little toe in your church, you have the same effect on your church (the body of Christ) as this man's little toe had on his body. The little toe has much to do with the balance of the body. If you're the little toe in your church, you have much to do with the balance of your church.

The little toe really doesn't have any effective muscles in it. If you lean off balance, and start to fall, your little toe has no muscles to stop you from falling. But it immediately sends a signal to the brain that says, "out of balance". Then the brain sends a signal to muscle number 642 in the right side of the foot to contract so your foot muscles can keep you from falling. My friend without a little toe had to pay great attention to what he was doing. If he ran, walked too fast, or if he wasn't paying attention, he'd lose his balance and fall. You may not even be the little toe, but you're still a very important part of the body. The worst thing you could do by being a little toe, is being a little toe that goes to sleep. The little toe that goes to sleep, just like the foot that goes to sleep, affects the whole body. You could be part of what's holding back your church.

Now What?

Everyone has needs. God has always used man to accomplish His plan. His plan is for everyone's needs to be met; therefore, His plan is for His people to meet the needs of others. Every person in the church should have a part in meeting the needs of people in the community and in the church. The responsibility then is to exercise the spiritual gift God has given in a TEAM effort with the rest of the diversely gifted body to meet all the needs of every person possible.

The more individual church members minister in this manner, the more balanced the church, the more lasting numerical and spiritual growth takes place and the more God is honored.

CHAPTER NINE

REVIEW QUESTIONS:

1. What is the two-fold purpose of the church?

2. Why is it important to meet people's needs in the church?

3. What is the end result of meeting all the needs of man as listed on the chart "Team Versus the Lost"?

DISCUSSION QUESTIONS:

1. How have some gifted people met needs in your life? What were the needs and who met them?

2. In what ways can the "biblical procedure" for training Christians help solve problems and meet needs in your life?

3. In what ways has your body been hampered when a part of the body did not function? What does that teach you about the church?

CHAPTER TEN

ABUSES OF THE TEAM GIFTS

The great violinist, Nicolo Paganini had thrilled audiences with his musical performances. His violin had been the source of melodies and harmonies impossible to describe in words. What joys the violin conveyed in the hands of the master. When he died, he willed his expensive and beautiful violin to the city of Genoa. The only condition was that it was never to be played again. The wood, since it was never used, decayed and became worm-eaten and useless. That beautifully toned instrument was grossly abused instead of providing the melodic tones for which it was intended. The same choice comes to the Christian with his spiritual gifts — he can use them or abuse them. The results are much the same as with the violin. They add beauty to life or sadness and uselessness.

God intended for the spiritual gifts to be used in carrying out the Great Commission and the edifying of the saints. When the gifts are misused or abused, they do not meet the needs of people in the family of God. Often, the TEAM pulls apart rather than pulling together. If we understand what abuses can take place, we can avoid them and concentrate our efforts on the task God gave us. Let's look at some terms that describe the misuses of spiritual gifts.

Gift Ignorance

Ignorance of spiritual gifts may be the major cause of much of the discouragement, insecurity, frustration and guilt that plagues many Christians, thereby holding back the effectiveness and growth of the church.

Ignorance of spiritual gifts is like the man who lived seven miles from Niagara Falls. A stranger asked if the roar that he heard was that of the great falls. The man replied that he wasn't really sure. He had never been there to see them. What a sight he missed by not traveling only seven miles to see them. The beauty of serving Christ with spiritual gifts can be missed simply because one never takes time to learn his gift and use it.

Gift Ignorance may be defined as a lack of knowledge regarding the possession of spiritual gifts and the nature of the gifts themselves by individual believers.

This lack of knowledge has evolved over the centuries from historical absence to modern abstinence. Whereas the forefathers gave us little material to study, the contemporary scholars have not addressed the task oriented (TEAM) gifts in their studies of the Holy Spirit.

Most contemporary scholars do agree that the doctrine of the Holy Spirit is one of (if not the) most important doctrines of Christianity. Churches lacking a sound scriptural teaching on this doctrine will also have problems on other doctrines as well.

Yet historians seem to verify that the doctrine has been under attack ever since the beginning of the Ante-Nicene period (AD 100) and almost totally suppressed during the Middle or Dark Ages (approximately 450-1517). John Walvoord states, "The Middle Ages on the whole were dark spiritually as well as intellectually, with few attaining any balance of doctrine acceptable to the earnest Bible student of today. Of the doctrine of the Holy Spirit in its entirety, there was practically no conception. Few grasped the need for personal conversion and the work of the Spirit in regeneration. Practically no attention was given to such subjects as the indwelling Spirit, the baptism of the Spirit, and the filling of the Spirit. It was expressly denied that the Spirit could teach all Christians through the Word of God. Earthly priests were substituted for the Holy Spirit. The 'things of the Spirit of God' were lost in the wilderness of sacramentarianism (salvation through the taking of sacraments), ignorance of the Word, superstition, humanism and scholasticism."[1]

Beginning with the Reformation, things began to change with Martin Luther's emphasis on the Spirit's work in regeneration and illumination and John Calvin's teaching the association of the Spirit and the Trinity. Other great contributions included John Owen's *Discourse Concerning the Holy Spirit* and Abraham Kuyper's *The Work of the Holy Spirit*. Kuyper's work was published in 1900, beginning this century's writings on the subject. But, most of the works before 1900 had almost nothing to say about the gifts of the Spirit unless it was to confuse them with the fruit and ministries of the Spirit, or a listing of the gifts with no theological *or* practical definition for the gift. Between 1900 and 1950, there was no practical application given.

Dr. Robert Lightner, Associate Professor of Systematic Theology at Dallas Theological Seminary sums it up best when he says, "Perhaps the most neglected area of the doctrine of the Holy Spirit has been the ministry of giving gifts to the members of Christ's Body."[2]

Most modern attention to gifts of the Holy Spirit has mainly centered on the "Miraculous Gifts", such as healing, tongues and miracles with very little, if any, emphasis on the "team gifts" (task oriented gifts). Although revival of the doctrine of spiritual gifts has been evident in this recent period, the abstinence of its application still remains evident.

Gift Blindness

Gift Blindness is a condition which results from "gift ignorance" and renders the victim incapable of recognizing his own spiritual gifts and their influence upon his own life and ministry.

Those afflicted with *gift blindness* may demonstrate a tendency to build doctrine around themselves, interpret Scripture in light of their own feelings or emotions and adjust their lifestyle to fulfill their personal desires. They are blind to the fact that their own emotions, desires, motivation and motives are influenced by their own spiritual gift. They become "Theo-methodologists" (the methodology that gives *them* fulfillment in life has become their theology).

The Theo-methodologist is often guilty of Bible-manipulation. Once his position is established, much effort is placed into finding verses to support the position. This is the opposite of the proper procedure of studying the Scripture, then establishing a position. In reality, he is building a doctrine around himself.

Years ago, I was in the sign business. Living near me was a man named Tony who had also been in the sign business. I was excited about what I was doing and could not understand why Tony was not excited about it any more. Every time I was around Tony, I would try to talk him into going back into the sign business. The problem was that I could not see why he was not as excited as I was about what excited me. We are often like that about our spiritual gifts. Those areas where we have spiritual gifts excite us and we need to realize that others who do not have the same gifts are not as excited about those areas as we are.

Gift blindness sometimes takes that form; it does not see the gifts that others have and how they too work for the glory of God. We must not be blind to our own gifts; we must not be blind to the gifts of others.

There is often a tendency to "beat people with the Bible" because others disagree with our position. The trend is to consider those who have other gifts to be less spiritual.

The accompanying diagram (Needs of the Ministry As Viewed by the Various Gifts) shows the importance that is put on the various areas of the ministry by the various members of the body. This emphasis is influenced by the motivation and desires of one's spiritual gifts. When a person is blind to the fact that his spiritual gifts provide such an influence on his life, it can create much frustration as he takes the most positive drives of his spiritual gifts and *imposes* them on others.

Gift Imposing

Gift Imposing is the act of forcing one's spiritual gift upon another and attempting to compel them to perform as though it was God's gift to them. Gift imposing wants the whole body to be an eye.

The activity of gift imposing is most frequently carried on by one who is suffering from "gift blindness". Such individuals fail to recognize the diversity of the body of Christ, and as a result, attempt to force other Christians to function in capacities for which God has not gifted them. They give the impression that they believe the area of ministry for which God has gifted and burdened them is superior to all others. In fact, some not only give the impression, but they "know" their gifts are the only ones that count — perhaps even the only ones in existence. "Gift imposers" distribute much frustration, discouragement and false guilt on others in the body of Christ.

Gift imposing involves "guilt-trip motivation" in imposing of gifts on others. People who practice it try to make others feel that they are not right with God unless they are involved with the same ministry as they are. For example, a person may have the gift of evangelism. He is motivated and consumed with personally leading people to Christ. He witnesses with tracts, talks to people on the street, in doctor's offices, on the bus or just anywhere and any time he can. Then he finds a fellow-Christian who has the gift of serving or showing mercy. Since the person is not out on the streets, "shaking the bushes" and confronting every

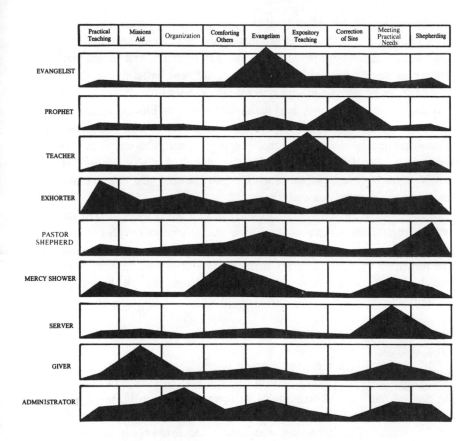

person he comes in contact with, the Evangelist accuses the person of not being burdened about souls. In reality, that may be far from the truth. The Mercy-shower may have been responsible for many coming to Christ because of his special ministry. The Server may have opened doors the Evangelist could only wish to be opened.

No believer who uses his gift properly should feel guilty for not having the same gift someone else has been given.

In the realm of leadership, *gift imposing* has taken a form which causes a serious threat to the unity of believers who do not go to the same church, but believe the same doctrine and share the same faith in God's Word. We have become so concerned (possibly to the point of obsession) with the authority of the pastor that any pastor not gifted as an administrator, exhorter or prophet is labeled as a compromiser and a failure. It makes no difference that he may function well in another gifted area, for he has led his church in a different pattern than those who have the gift of administrator, prophet or exhorter.

In reality, the pastor may best maintain the proper Biblical authority by delegating organizational responsibility to a person with the gift of administration and the motivational functions to an exhorter. A pastor does not need to feel guilt for leading his church that way. Pastors as well as laymen should properly exercise their spiritual gifts in a manner that best promotes the cause of Christ.

In the church, gift imposers "impose" in two basic ways: first, with and because of the burden of their own hearts; secondly with the one string banjo, where week in and week out, the same message is restated and presented again. This drives many away and makes the ones who stay think that the one thing continuously emphasized is all there is to the ministry.

Gift Gravitation

Gift gravitation refers to the tendency among Christians to attract and be attracted to other Christians with like spiritual gifts. It grows out of the natural tendency of individuals to form bonds with those of like interests and aspirations (the Homogeneous Unit). Certainly, there is nothing wrong with fellowship with others and exchanging ideas and plans for using our gifts, but we must be careful not to form cliques and exclude others with differing gifts.

Gift Colonization

Gift Colonization is the direct and inescapable result of unrestrained "gift gravitation". "Gift gravitation" is perfectly normal and a result of human nature and the need to be accepted by those who are similar to us (our peers). *Gift colonization* is the extreme. The real problem comes when our failure to recognize that we are colonizing, and then attacking those who are not the same as we are.

"Gift Gravitation" is the *process* which is usually practiced by the layman and "gift colonization" is the *result*, which is usually unwittingly sustained by the leadership.

When it comes to colonization, possibly the strongest magnetism drawing people together is values. Spiritual gifts influence values which in turn lead people with those gifts to gravitate to one another. However, in most cases, those guilty of gift colonization have only a superficial awareness of spiritual gifts and their function (gift ignorance).

The negative result of colonization is that many pastors quit preaching *to* their congregations, and start preaching *at* the congregation down the street or on the other side of town or the nation. Once colonization takes place it is easier to preach at the other guy. Every Sunday morning the sermon is not what his church should be doing, but what the other church, or group of churches (movement) shouldn't be doing. This causes his own congregation to feel cozy, self-righteous and complacent.

Over the years, there has been increasing evidence of *gift colonization* in the major church movements in America. Careful observation of these movements reveals that their characteristics, strengths, weaknesses, ministry emphasis and leadership styles correlate with the characteristics of certain spiritual gifts. Such correlations lead to acceptance of doctrines and philosophies which support those characteristics, therefore making their colonization even stronger. We have come to a point where we must admit that spiritual gifts are a major factor in the undeliberate formation of the individual movements. I am not saying that everyone in each movement has the same gift. On the contrary all gifts are present in each movement, but certain spiritual gifts are more evident and have become dominant in each movement. I also recognize there are many similarities among all the movements. I am not inferring or stating that everyone with these gifts is guilty of this kind of colonization, nor that everyone within these movements has the same gifts. I am simply saying that when carried to excess, such trends are evident.

All of the movements have strengths which have a tendency to draw even more of the same spiritual gifts into their movement. Thus more *gift colonization* takes place.

When someone within a movement has a particular gift that is not part of the *gift colonization* for that movement, they are forced to either gravitate to another movement or misuse their gift. For example, a person with the gift of evangelism who is in a non-evangelistic movement may find himself proselyting in order to fulfill the motivation of his gift.

However, because of the lack of an evangelistic emphasis within his own movement he may attempt to win people to his philosophy rather than the Body of Christ.

In the following list, notice the dominant characteristics of churches produced by *gift colonization*. Careful attention will aid you in understanding how colonization relates to the major movements, and how the characteristics of the gifts correlate to the dominant characteristics of the churches within each movement.

The *Evangelist* — builds Back-door churches; many converts, many "deserters" out the back door.

The *Prophet* — builds Legalistic churches; much control over individual lives and close monitoring of members' behavior.

The *Teacher* — builds Intellectual churches; theologians, much Bible study, content oriented.

The *Exhorter* — builds Deeper-life churches; personal edification emphasis.

The *Pastor/Teacher* — builds Maintenance oriented churches; much shepherding follow-up, and caretaking.

The *Giver* — builds Mission oriented churches; home and foreign support raised.

The *Mercy Shower* — builds Emotional churches; affectionate, tears and smiles; much worship.

The *Server* — builds Humanitarian churches; community awareness, help poor and under-privileged.

The *Administrator* — builds doctrinally Shallow churches; many committees, well-organized, many programs, but may lack spiritual and doctrinal depth.

Gift Coveting

Gift coveting is the activity of desiring a gift other than that which has been given to the individual by the Holy Spirit. This will lead to frustration and a lack of fulfillment since God's true purpose for us is not ever achieved.

The Mercy Shower should not wish for the gift of evangelism, but use the gift he has to touch and soften hearts. The Prophet should not wish for the gift of serving so that he would be better liked. Let the Server keep the building in good repair so the Prophet can spend his time in prayer and Bible study and preaching. Let each one carry his part of the load and allow the other person to carry his. Many times Christians waste their lives wishing they were someone else. God knew who could be trusted with which gifts, so he placed them in the proper hands (see I Corinthians 12:18; John 15:16).

Care should be exercised in distinguishing between gift coveting and the natural desire of the gift one has. If there is a strong desire for a gift which was not shown as one of the gifted areas when taking the Spiritual Gift Profile, or if there is not a strong desire in one which was indicated as a possessed gift, the Profile may need to be taken again. Since a spiritual gift is partially defined as a supernatural desire, the gift will automatically be a part of the desire of the believer.

Once the gifted areas are defined and affirmed, one will need to exercise care about envying someone else's gifted area. The distinction must also be made between gifted areas and the practice of Christian attitudes and traits every believer should exercise. For example, everyone should give, show mercy, serve and witness.

How To Avoid Abuses

The best deterrent to abusing spiritual gifts is *education*. Christians must not suffer from "gift ignorance" or it will definitely lead into other abuses. All the abuses are a form of "gift ignorance". Pastors must teach and preach the "whole counsel of God" in the area of spiritual gifts.

There are basically three areas of education needed. First, Christians must be educated concerning what *a* spiritual gift is. Secondly, they must be educated concerning what their *own* spiritual gifts are. Third, they must be educated concerning what other Christians' spiritual gifts are and how those gifts relate to their own gifts. Of course, they must learn how this all fits into the Biblical concept of TEAM ministry.

The education concerning spiritual gifts must combat "gift ignorance" in believers by covering the first two areas (what a gift is and what their gifts are). "Gift blindness" is avoided by the teaching concerning other Christians' gifts. "Gift imposing" is an extreme of this blindness when the believer not only misuses his own gift, but forces others to function within the wrong gift capacity. By teaching the balance of the body as taught in I Corinthians 12, Romans 12 and Ephesians 4:16, "gift imposing" can be avoided. As I mentioned earlier, "gift gravitation" is perfectly natural until it becomes extreme, especially to the point of "colonization". This extreme can be avoided by teaching the necessity of having all the gifts in the church so the church as a body can meet the needs of the community and the local church body. "Gift coveting" is avoided when a believer knows his gift and functions within the body properly with that gift. When he is fulfilled serving in such a position in the church, he has no desire for someone else's gift.

Now What?

When the TEAM Gifts are abused or misused, the entire body of the church suffers. The balance is lost and the work of God is adversely affected. To carry any strength to an extreme is to make it a weakness. All of the abuses are simply strengths carried to an extreme, through "riding a hobby horse", or through a lack of understanding that God did not want everybody to be the same and have the same gifts. God makes everyone different both on the outside (some tall, some short; some skinny, some fat; some blonde, brunette or redhead; some dark-skinned, some light-skinned, etc.) and the inside (some prophets, some evangelists, some administrators, some mercy showers, etc. with the various desires and motives characteristic of those gifts). It is easier to recognize the outer differences than the inner differences. Just as we do not belittle a man who is 5' 2" for not wearing a size 48 coat, we should not criticize a prophet for not being a mercy shower, or any other gifted person for not practicing someone else's gift.

The more the Christian matures, the more he will learn to mix with people with differing gifts and to accept the differing motives, desires and needs. He must learn to be part of the TEAM rather than being an individual who must "win the world" on his own. One person does not build a church, one gift does not meet all the needs, one individual does not reach and teach a generation. We must TEAM together and complement each other instead of trying to give everyone the same gift and the same part in the task.

CHAPTER TEN

REVIEW QUESTIONS:

1. What is "gift imposing" and how does it affect the work of God?

2. Which abuse can lead to "gift blindness" if carried to extremes? Why?

3. How do "gift gravitation" and "gift colonization" work?

DISCUSSION QUESTIONS:

1. What kind of problems would you find in a church with heavy gift colonization? What kind of advantages?

2. Which church in the list of colonized churches would you feel most comfortable in and why?

3. How have you personally suffered as a result of "gift abuses"? What did you learn from the situation? What effect did it have on you and your spiritual life? (Do not use people's names.)

FOOTNOTES:

[1] Walvoord, John F., *The Holy Spirit* (Zondervan Publishing House: Grand Rapids, 1954/1958) Page 246.

[2] Lightner, Robert P., *Speaking in Tongues and Divine Healing* (Regular Baptist Press: Schaumburg, 1965/1978) Page 10.

CHAPTER ELEVEN

THE GIFT OF EVANGELISM AND ITS RELATIONSHIP
TO EVANGELISM

The score is tied, the bases are loaded, it's the bottom of the ninth. The past two batters have gone down swinging — tension is at a peak — pressure is on to make the most important decision of this championship series. The coach in the dugout decides on a pinch hitter to bat in this crucial situation. He must make the right choice. The coach encourages his clutch player to do his best, "You can do it; just be a man and do what we need you to do. We're counting on you to do your job. Go to it and get it done." Out of the shadows of the dugout comes the man he has sent to the plate — the team's best starting *pitcher*, who only has a batting average of .097 — the *weakest* hitter on the team.

The success of each team will ultimately rest on the ability and foresight of the coach putting the right player in the right position at the right time. That's where it always rests. Coaches must know their players and their skills, how they react to certain situations and what they can do under pressure. Success in business depends on proper use of personnel. The two most important elements of personnel usage are placing those best suited to each position and each player being part of the team. Teamwork requires everyone doing their best at their position with their skills and cooperating with the others doing the same thing. It is called "Workforce Economics".

So it is in the church. The pastor is like the coach of a ball team; Christ is the owner; the members are the players. The owner expects the coach to "manage" the team in such a way as to use the best qualified players in the proper positions and teach them to work together as a team in such a manner as to "win the game". Winning the game in the church is reaching our communities for Christ and bringing the new converts and church members to full maturity — *reaching* and *teaching*.

There are strengths and deficiencies in every area of the ministry, but these deficiencies are probably more evident in the area of evangelism than anywhere else. In this one area alone, our "coaches" have inflicted more guilt, frustration and discouragement by expecting all the players to perform like the team's best hitter.

Possibly the greatest contribution the Church Growth Movement has made to spiritual gifts is recognizing and properly defining the gift of evangelism. Understanding of this gift is imperative to proper understanding of the relationship of spiritual gifts to church growth.

To properly understand spiritual gifts' relationship to evangelism, we must first understand the difference between the gift of evangelism and the command to evangelize. Let's take a look at both.

The Command To Evangelize

There are two basic positions on evangelism which dominate Christianity. Although a variety of Scriptures are used for their support, both positions would view their interpretation of the Great Commission as their foundation. (Matthew 28:18-20, Mark 16:15-18, Luke 24:47-48, John 20:21-23, and Acts 1:8).

Position #1 *Confrontation Evangelism*: The interpretation of these combined Scriptures says that every Christian has the responsibility to witness to every unsaved person. Furthermore, witnessing goes beyond the personal testimony, requiring a presentation of the Gospel and pursuing a decision. This leads to the belief that God's primary objective in saving sinners is to make them soul-winners.

Most people holding this position contend that the Great Commission was given to the individual, not to the church, and that we all have a personal responsibility to fulfill it. When speaking of the Great Commission, they most often quote the passage in Mark and emphasize "preach the Gospel to every creature." They believe that soul-winning is the most important work a person can do.

This position generally rejects the idea that God has given a gift that would enable certain Christians to become more effective or aggressive soul-winners than others, therefore removing any and all excuses of the "un-gifted" for not soul-winning. Most believe that evangelism in Ephesians 4 is a calling of God and an office of the church and therefore given to those called into full-time evangelistic ministries (for example, D. L. Moody, Billy Sunday, John R. Rice, Billy Graham, etc.). Their belief, as they communicate it, is that God will enable any yielded person to overcome the obstacles that would hinder him from becoming the kind of soul-winner they themselves are.

Within this first position are two extremes or variations. One extreme would say things like: "If you are not winning two or three souls a week, maybe you should question your own salvation." Or, "The evidence of the fullness of the Holy Spirit is not whether you are speaking in tongues but rather, how many souls you are winning to Christ." (All Scripture supported, of course.)

The other would say, "The Scriptures don't say you have to get results; you only have to sow seeds." This leads to a simplified three-point tract that enables you to present the Gospel to a hundred homes on a Saturday afternoon without any need for follow-up.

Both extremes have messages entitled "Go" and use the passage in Acts saying "house to house", assuring us that this was the way they did it in the early church; therefore, it's the *only* successful way for us to evangelize today. Both are heavy users of tracts but would insist that they should never be used as a "cop-out" to personal witnessing. Many times they leave the Christian feeling unspiritual or inferior because he is not a member of the visitation program.

Both of these extremes often border on "Easy-Believe-ism" (decision getting without true conversion) and "Guilt-trip Evangelism" (motivation by guilt).

Position #2, *Lifestyle Evangelism*: This position is quite the opposite of the first. Their reaction to the heavy emphasis on soul-winning gives the Great Commission a different twist. They stress the passage in Matthew and point out that the Commission really emphasizes teaching, which they do well. They would agree that the Great Commission conveys the idea that all should be witnesses — and a witness is "living your life that others might see Christ in you." You may hear one say, "Our job is to sow seeds, but not verbal seeds, for actions speak louder than words."

Many holding this position would say that the gift of evangelism *is* an office of the church, therefore making it the duty of the paid staff to do the evangelizing. Still others would say, "The gift of evangelism is available to all, but I don't have it," therefore relieving themselves of the responsibility of sharing the Gospel with others.

This group will accuse the first group of being over-zealous and offering an overly simplified plan for salvation, while they themselves have a very complicated and theological explanation for God's redemption of man.

An extreme for this position slides into the hyper-Calvinism philosophy.

The big problem with Lifestyle Evangelism is that it is a philosophy based on an over-reaction to Confrontational Evangelism. Therefore, the problem with Lifestyle Evangelism is not its philosophy or methodology, but the attitude in which it was conceived. A person holding either of the two positions must evaluate his own attitude for holding that position.

Evaluation Of Both Positions

It is noteworthy that both positions are built basically on *their* interpretation of the Great Commission. It is also important to acknowledge that both positions have good scriptural arguments, although neither side would agree with such a statement about the other.

The most important thing to notice about both positions is they fit the gifts, personalities, motivations, temperaments, character strengths and weaknesses of each group.

We must recognize each position for what it is — a *method*, not a scriptural mandate. It is a method that basically fits the dominant gift of each group. Both positions border on becoming "Theo-methodologists".

It is not our place to condemn either position. Both are effective. But the attitude that says *everyone* should fit into *their* position is wrong. Some people, either by gift or personality, can never become an outgoing or confrontational person. While others, because of their gift or personality, would never be able to "give testimony only" by their actions —they must be outgoing and verbal.

Balance Is The Answer

A third position, that of "TEAM Ministry", is also one that has a valid scriptural interpretation. It not only fits Scripture but also fits the personalities of all Christians, not just one group. This position recognizes individuals, acknowledging that some men are without complexes: men who know no fear, men who can use any method under any situation, with anyone, and win them to Christ.

It recognizes that a method suitable to this personality would be "over the head" of the average Christian. It recognizes that few people have the above outstanding qualities. It also recognizes that most Christians are timid, and an attempt at direct confrontational soul-winning is an overwhelming experience for them.

The Position Of TEAM Evangelism

1) God has given to some Christians (it appears to be approximately 10%)[1] the gift of Evangelism which endows them to be effective and confrontational while leading people to Christ. This gift can manifest itself through mass evangelism (preaching to groups) or through personal confrontational witnessing one-on-one, pursuing a decision.

2) God at the same time gives *every* Christian the responsibility to be a *witness.*

It is important to recognize here that the largest difference in the functions of these two groups is the methods, not the results of each. The witness has the responsibility to take advantage of the opportunities God provides for him to actively present the gospel, while the evangelist has the responsibility to make the opportunities for himself. It is important to recognize that a fine line exists as to what may be called an opportunity. However, we must allow this decision to be made in the heart of the person being faced with the situation, for he alone will be responsible before God as to how he used or did not use the situation.

This position does not relieve Christians from reaching out to a lost world with the gospel, but only acknowledges that God endows some people to do this through methods that may not fit all people.

The Bottom Line

The bottom line comes in actual practice of the principles, not in their interpretation.

1) *Every Christian should evangelize in one manner or another.* You can be a soul-winner without being a "soul-winner". I remember a young woman in my home church several years ago. The Pastor and Evangelist were trying to motivate our members to "go out and win the lost". She was in my Sunday School class, and she told me, "If they think I'm going to go out and get people saved, they're crazy, because I just can't do it." Yet that very evening, she and her husband were responsible for having 26 visitors in the service. Several of them accepted

Christ on the invitation. Was she a soul-winner or not? She didn't think she was. However, she was doing the work of an evangelist, but not through direct confrontation which she thought was expected of her.

2) *God has endowed some Christians with the gift of evangelism* that will enable them, more so than others, to function more effectively within the boundaries of the methodology used in the average visitation program.

3) *God has not called everyone to be a part of the visitation program* . A person God has not called to be a part of it should not have to bear the burden of guilt nor be made to feel unspiritual or inadequate because he is not practicing that type of evangelism.

Guilt is not always a motivator, but quite often a tool of Satan for destruction. Most guilt only suppresses efficiency. A distinction must be made between the guilt associated with the Holy Spirit convicting one of sin, and the false guilt placed by man when one does not live up to another man's expectations. The guilt from the Holy Spirit is associated with conviction. If the principle being conveyed is not for that person or the teaching is not valid, the Holy Spirit will not convict. One must be careful not to attempt to do the Holy Spirit's work for Him.

Studies done in the Church Growth Movement indicate that approximately ten percent of Christians have the gift of evangelism.[1] That suggests that ninety percent do not have that gift, indicating the presence of some other gift in their lives. The real problem is that only five percent of those *with the gift of evangelism* are actually leading sinners to Christ. In other words, one-half of one percent of the total church population is actually playing any part in leading people to Christ. To put it another way, ninety-nine and one-half percent of the people in the church are not evangelizing.

The problem occurs when the blame is placed on the ninety-nine and one-half percent for not evangelizing. The blame should be put on the ninety-five percent of the gifted evangelists who are not fulfilling their mission and calling. They are primarily the ones God has called to do the job. Perhaps if this were done, the other ninety percent who have differing gifts could feel the freedom to put those gifts to work. The result would be better "Workforce Economics" and more effectiveness as a TEAM for evangelism and growing churches.

4) *Balance needs to be taught when it comes to evangelism*. Teach that there is a difference in people and in methodology. Help each Christian

find where he fits in so he can effectively help the lost person take another step towards making that decision for Christ. One may not be able to directly confront someone with the Gospel and obtain a decision from them, but that person can play a part in bringing a person one step closer to accepting Christ.

5) *Understand fear as an excuse.*

Everyone can laugh at this cartoon, but in reality, for most of us it strikes close to home.

Fear is a hush-hush subject. It's something we all have, yet we don't want anyone else to know. And because others are afraid to mention it, we think they don't have any fear, thus making us believe we are the only ones who do. I took a speech class once. I was surprised with the boldness with which the instructor talked about fear while all the students sat there acting as if they didn't know what he was talking about. All the while they were shaking in their shoes, knowing he was going to call on one of them soon to stand in front of the class and make a speech.

I have a friend who worked for the telephone company. We were riding along in the car one day when he suddenly pointed and said, "See that pole — pole number 628743? I'll never forget that one. It's the one we worked on the first day I worked for the phone company ten years ago. I was scared to death."

I quickly answered, saying, "You mean they made you climb a telephone pole the first day you worked for them?"

"No," he said. "I was afraid they were going to ask me to climb one."

Preaching on fear will never get many amens. The fearless think the preacher is crazy or making excuses for the fearful and the fearful are too afraid to shout "Amen."

In Revelation 21:8 the fearful are listed as the number one inhabitants of Hell — those who were scared to profess faith in Christ for fear of ridicule or of what others would think. If this is so, how many had enough courage to just step over the line? They had enough courage to be saved, but no farther. Fear is not something that can be preached away. This usually only leads to frustration on the part of the fearful party. The presence of fear must be equally balanced with understanding and practical application, or "how to" type teaching, in order to overcome fear. Knowledge brings self-confidence and self-confidence will eradicate much of the fear because of knowing one can face what he fears.

Therefore, TEAM Evangelism teaches that every Christian, both new and old, should take an active part in a personal evangelism training class. When the instructors are thoughtful, they can train without scaring the student to death or putting him in embarrassing situations.

This training can do two things for the church: First, those who do not have the gift of evangelism will soon learn so. Yet, the practical teaching will help them overcome much of their fear. This makes it easier for them to *witness* to others while they minister in another capacity, using the gift God has given them. Secondly, those that have the gift of evangelism will soon develop a stronger burden for winning the lost. I am convinced that no one can sit through practical teaching of the gift God has given him without soon getting a burden from God with the conviction and motivation to perform the task.

Fear may still be present after the training but God will give the motivation needed to overcome it.

6) *Perhaps the greatest hindrance to witnessing comes in lack of discipline.* One must *force* himself to carry out the responsibilities of his gift and his duty to witness. Habits must be formed that place him in the opportunities that best suit his gift and abilities. When he fails to take advantage of opportunities when he definitely has freedom of the Holy Spirit to witness, he develops a pattern of missed opportunities. Proper

training in an effective evangelism course will help to set those practices and the self-discipline necessary to be the most effective.

The Conclusion of the Matter

"Your material on gifts is great. Why don't you leave the 'Sacred Cow' (meaning the gift of evangelism) alone like everyone else? Without that controversy, everyone would accept it!" More than once I have been asked a similar question.

This material is based on helping Christians discover their gifts and find fulfillment in life through the use of those gifts. Teaching new truths and mixing them with old misconceptions will only confuse and frustrate people even more. A person can never be led to be effective and fulfilled doing what he should be doing if he is living under guilt, because he is not doing what he *thinks* he should be doing. You see, *it's not what you are that holds you back — it's what you think you're not.*

The reason for non-involvement goes far beyond lack of commitment. Possibly the greatest hindrance to effective evangelism the church has done to itself by first looking at the task, secondly, looking at the qualifications to fulfill the task and third, attempting to make everyone in the local church qualify. The leadership tells the team, "I know you're a good first baseman or shortstop, but that's of secondary importance because everyone on our team must first be a good recruiter." With that attitude continuing, our current team members are either going to leave the team or join the ranks of the majority and become a spectator.

We must never forget that every year, it's not the club with the best recruiter, the best pitcher or the best shortstop that takes home the pennant — but the one with the best TEAM.

Now What?

Nowhere does the value of God's plan for spiritual gifts come into focus than in the total process of evangelism and outreach. The guilt must be removed from those who are serving God in their gifted areas. Again, teamwork is essential in order to be most effective. In this area more than possibly any other, Christians have been guilty of gift imposing. Guilt has been imposed on those who do not live up to the expectations of someone else. It is difficult to live up to what God expects, but it is ten times more difficult to live up to what others often expect. God equips people to live up to His expectations, but man does not.

Different people have taken different approaches to evangelism because of their backgrounds or spiritual gifts and the influences on their lives. It is necessary for the believer to realize that if God has not gifted him in certain areas, he should not force himself to be what he is not, but to work as God has gifted him. Then he must TEAM up with those of differing gifts so they can *together* reach this generation with the gospel, win them to Christ, and teach them how to mature and grow into a complete Christian. The believer can be more effective by being himself than by trying to be someone else.

The church must evangelize! Every believer must become involved somewhere in the process of evangelizing, as part of the TEAM. In other words, your spiritual gift may relieve you from the responsibility of confrontational evangelism, but it will never relieve you from the responsibility to evangelize.

FOOTNOTES:

1 Wagner, C. Peter, *Your Spiritual Gifts Can Help Your Church Grow* (Regal Books, Glendale: 1979) Page 177.

CHAPTER ELEVEN

REVIEW QUESTIONS:

1. Describe "Workforce Economics".

2. What are the three positions on evangelism?

3. What is the key to the TEAM Evangelism position as outlined?

DISCUSSION QUESTIONS:

1. How has the "confrontation" method of witnessing affected your own ministry? Which of the three positions would make you most comfortable? Why?

2. How can people overcome the greatest hindrance to witnessing?

3. How are the definitions of witnessing affecting you and what changes does the new definition bring to mind for you?

CHAPTER TWELVE

FINDING YOUR PLACE ON THE TEAM

Sir Michael Costa, the celebrated conductor, was holding a rehearsal. As the mighty chorus rang out, accompanied by scores of instruments, the piccolo player thought perhaps he could quit playing without being missed since there was so much music being played. Suddenly the great leader stopped and cried out: "Where is the piccolo?" The sound of that one small instrument was necessary for the full harmony of the piece and the conductor's ear had missed it when it did not play. So it is with the individual's spiritual gift. Every part must be played, every gift must be used or the whole will suffer. *You are important!*

We all have heroes in the work of God, people we consider great and outstanding because of their positions and accomplishments. Stop for a moment and think of the most outstanding Christian leader or teacher you know. Don't go on until you have a name. Have one? Now consider this: God has called you to do something he or she *cannot* do. God has called you to do something that your pastor can't do. He's called you to do something that your favorite evangelist can't do, regardless of how great he is. Your church needs you in order to fulfill its mission in the community where God placed it. God has called you, "little ole you", to do something that only you can do. The task may have seemed small to you in the past, but it is big as far as God is concerned. And just as importantly, that is all God has called you to be accountable for. You will never be called to account for God's calling on someone else's life.

In order to fill that special place in His ministry, you need to know what that special place is. Here are some simple steps to follow.

What NOT To Do.

Before we can understand what we are *to do*, it would behoove us to look at what we are *not to do*.

Avoid the abuses and misuses of spiritual gifts (see Chapter 10). It is easy to fall into these traps laid by Satan. He has always specialized in causing people to go to extremes with good things and in so doing, cause those good things to become bad. Much of the guilt associated with Christian work is not conviction from the Holy Spirit, but false guilt caused by not living up to men's expectations. You must make your personal ministry a real matter of prayer, allowing God to reveal to you the real position you occupy in His work. Don't allow men to impose their gifts on you; don't gravitate or colonize with those with like gifts and become a group of people who do not fit with others who have other gifts; don't be blind to others' gifts; don't be ignorant of your gift nor the gifts of others; don't covet gifts God gave to someone else. He made no mistake when He gave yours to you (I Corinthians 12:18).

Avoid impulsive decisions. Many Bible college and seminary students make the rash mistake of quitting school to become involved in the "more glamorous" ministry, damaging their futures for what seemed to be a great opportunity for serving the Lord. It was a impulsive decision based on feelings and desire more than on God's leadership and plan for success in their lives. They may succeed for a while, but sooner or later, they are frustrated in their efforts to serve Christ. Many laymen do the same thing concerning their spiritual gifts. They choose their ministry based on their feelings or some speaker's passionate cry rather than taking the time to see where they really fit in and what their real gift is.

Be yourself. I don't want to imply that you can't serve God without knowing the name of your spiritual gifts. Some people have never heard of spiritual gifts and have been effectively serving God for many years. Yet many suddenly think they have to get a new position to fit their newly found gift. Stop and consider — you might be where God wants you and you don't need to make any changes whatsoever. *The expression of the gift is more important than the title or name.* Make sure your decisions are thought through carefully before you make any changes of ministry.

Avoid "gift obsession". Don't substitute gifts for a spirit-filled life. Don't make the mistake of making spiritual gifts an end in themselves. They are only a means to an end. This was a problem to the Corinthians. They substituted the spirit-filled life with spiritual gifts. *A steady diet of any one thing will always cause malnutrition.* Continue studying doctrine, evangelism, church growth principles and most importantly, the Bible. The key word is *balance* for usefulness in the work of God.

Another entire study could be done on balance and the priorities that God has set for our lives. I believe that God has five priorities for our lives: God first (the foundation on which to build everything else), family second, your ministry third, your work fourth, and yourself fifth.

Remember, in the relationship of spiritual gifts to the will of God, the first six principles are the spirit-filled life: to be saved, sanctified, spirit-filled, submissive, suffering and serving. Serving (the practice of spiritual gifts) was only one part of the spirit-filled life. We need to be careful that we don't take gifts out of that perspective.

Avoid "gift dodging". In his book *Is My Church What God Meant It To Be?*, Gary Hauck writes, "Do not neglect other responsibilities by hiding behind your spiritual gift! How often I have heard someone say, 'Oh, no, I don't witness. Evangelism just isn't my spiritual gift!' While it is true that God hasn't given a special unusual ability in evangelism to every Christian, *every Christian* is responsible to evangelize! Paul even told Timothy, who had the gift of pastor-teacher to 'do the work of an evangelist' (II Timothy 4:5).

"In the same way, Christians who do not possess the gift of giving are responsible to uphold the work of God financially, and Christians who do not have the gift of helps are nevertheless responsible to 'do good unto all men.' We must not hide behind our spiritual gifts. We are to excel in the area of our gift, but we are not free from responsibility in the other areas of service."[1]

What TO Do

First, you should *learn to perform all the gifts.* You might say, "You mean you have taken me this far, through all these distinctions on the gifts, all these separations on the gifts, all these characteristics on the gifts, and now you tell me I have to learn *every one* of them?" Let me explain. Throughout the Bible you will find many Scriptures that give you the commands to perform all these functions. Just calling yourself a Christian (Christ like) implies such a life. Christ is a perfect example of all the gifts and exemplifies the need for you to learn to perform in every gift. But, let's not stop here. Read on.

Excel in one or more. This is the real key in gift usage. Yes, you need to learn to perform all the gifts. There are times in your life when you will have to confront sin like a prophet and you will have to be practical like an exhorter, and you will have to study like a teacher, and you will have to comfort somebody like a mercy shower; there are times you will have to be a leader; there are times you will have to do service in the church. You might not like many of these tasks, but there are times you will have to do them. But the point is, find the dominant gift God has given you and that's the one where you want to *excel*. That's the one in which you want to wrap up your whole life. That's right, put all your eggs in one basket and give the basket to God. Don't try to be a super-man and develop all the gifts. You will never be able to. Most people are able to develop at the most, two or three gifts. Take your dominant gift and develop it. That is the one where you should excel, and that's the one to make your personal ministry.

HOW IT'S DONE

This is the actual "how-to discover your spiritual gift" procedure.

Prayer. Ask God daily to reveal to you your spiritual gift. You should make this a matter of prayer until you are sure that you understand what your spiritual gift is or what calling God has for your life.

Examine carefully the characteristics section of this book. It will help you in determining what your gift is as you evaluate how each character-istic relates to you. Also, Church Growth Institute has a test available for a nominal fee that will help you come to grips with your gift (See Order Page in back of this text.)

Seek the help of a more mature Christian who has been educated on the principles and uses of spiritual gifts. Let me emphasize, *who has been educated on the principles and uses of spiritual gifts.* A lot of people who are willing to help you with your spiritual gifts have only a superficial awareness themselves as to what spiritual gifts are. They really can't help you, because they don't fully understand gifts either. Evaluate your answers to the questions from Chapter One with him. However, keep in mind that there are two kinds of people that evaluate their church. The kind that says, "What *we* need to do is. . ." usually is an individual who is willing to help. And then there is the other kind that says, "What *you* need to do is. . ." Usually, he is just a complainer who wants to get something off his chest. Be a "We" person, not a "You" person.

Discard the obvious gifts. After going through this material, you now recognize that you obviously don't have some of these gifts. Discard them. Don't forget the necessity to fulfill the normal Christian role of the gifts counterpart but don't seek to make any of those gifts your area of ministry.

Select three that you might have. Several people teach that you only have one spiritual gift based on the word "the", in II Timothy 1:6 where Paul says to, "Stir up *the* gift of God which is in thee." On the other hand some teach that all Christians have all the gifts but in varying degrees of intensity. Scripture does not support either position. In I Corinthians 12:29, Paul asks, "Are all apostles? are all prophets? are all teachers?" The obvious answer to his series of questions is "no." Therefore, no one can have all the gifts. But, if you want to take sides, take sides with the second position, because chances are you have several gifts that will vary in different degrees and intensity. You might have two or three gifts and one of them will be more dominant than the others. Another may quote "Every man hath his proper gift of God," referring to I Corinthians 7:7. I believe the word "proper" refers to your dominant gift although other gifts will obviously be present. This makes a wide variety and combination of characteristics or motives that will be evident in you. One teacher calls it your gift mix,[2] but it's really a combination of several spiritual gifts in varying degrees.

Begin functioning on the "Team." This is the most important principle in determining your gift. You can study spiritual gifts from now on and you will never discover what your spiritual gift is until you get involved. You must start serving God before you can really discover your gift. You have to get a ship moving before you can steer it. Be available.

Begin functioning in areas correlating with the three gifts revealed in your evaluation. Work as a helper. Go to your pastor and explain what you are trying to do. Say, "Pastor, I would like to become involved with a short term project connected with (whatever area you are trying)." Or, "May I work in the nursery for a month? I'd like to drive a bus for a month," or "I'd like to teach during the week of Vacation Bible School in the children's department." Or, "I'll help visit during the 4 Saturdays of the promotion." Or whatever might appeal to you. It is especially easy to do relief work in different areas during the summer when people have to be gone due to vacations. The key though is not to obligate yourself permanently. Don't say, "Pastor, I think I have the gift of teaching. Will you give me a Sunday School class to teach forever?" If you misinterpreted, you will burn yourself out. Move around at first. Explain to the pastor why you want to move around and that you are willing to be a helper. Most pastors should cooperate and help you by introducing you to the leaders in these areas. As you work in these positions, you will get a feel for whether you fit in or not. When does the hand know it's a hand? When it does the work of a hand. When does a foot know when it's a foot? When it is doing what a foot does. And the same is true with you. Get involved in the body; get on the "Team". This is the only way you will truly discover your spiritual gift.

Look for satisfied desires, results, and recognition. Some people say, "I have the gift of teaching, the problem is nobody in my class has the gift of learning." If nobody in your class has the gift of learning then chances are you don't have the gift of teaching, or you haven't taken the time to develop it. Because everyone who has the gift of teaching will be able to present material that will create some change in the lives of other people. Watch for some satisfaction about what you are doing. If there is none, it is the wrong job for you.

If you don't enjoy what you are doing, you are not in the will of God. Remember that God did not call you to a life of misery. The Christian is not to "grin and bear it". He did not call you to do a life of menial tasks, serving in areas that will never bring you any fulfillment. God wants you to live a fulfilled life and your spiritual gift is the source of joy in your Christian life as you use it to serve God.

Spiritual Gifts And Their Relationship To Your Secular Employment

Spiritual gifts were given for the work of the ministry. In many cases, however, they may complement your "secular employment", your job which you have in order to provide for your family. It is very possible that your spiritual gifts can allow you to perform more efficiently in all areas of your life. Highest performance in every area of life is part of your testimony to God's leadership.

Ephesians 4:1 says, "I therefore the prisoner of the Lord, beseech you that ye walk worthy of the vocation wherewith you are called." What is a vocation? Our present terminology would say it's your job. But not so biblically. Your vocation is your total life's calling. It includes every aspect of your life, including your occupation (your job), your avocation (your hobby), your family and your ministry. The problem is most Christians want to treat their vocation like it was their avocation —

serving God in their religion on Sundays. Serving God, for the true Christian, is a full-time job taking in every God-given priority. It should never be treated as a hobby.

There was a man who had a large and successful tomato farm. He had several hundred acres of tomatoes and sold them to the large food processing companies. He also was very active in Christian endeavors, especially in Sunday School. In fact, he taught a large class of adults and was well-known as a Bible teacher. One day, someone asked him, "How can you find the time to teach and shepherd such a large Sunday School class with all your business affairs and other things to be responsible for?" His reply was, "Sunday School *is* my business. I grow tomatoes to pay the bills." Such should be the attitude of the Christian.

Often, knowing a person's spiritual gifts can help in setting a career path which is both enjoyable and a witness at the same time. For example, the evangelist may make a good salesman; the exhorter may make a good writer of training manuals or an instructor for training purposes; the administrator may make a good manager or supervisor in certain situations.

The worst abuse in this area is when your spiritual gift is used in your employment *only* and not in the work of God. Let me illustrate.

If I gave one of my staff $40 and said, "Take your wife to dinner and have an evening of enjoyment at my expense," I would expect him to do just that with my gift. If he took the money and bought gas and groceries and went home and watched TV, he misused my gift. However, if he bought $5 worth of gas in order to take his wife out to dinner at a nice restaurant, it was not an abuse of the gift. Buying the gas enabled him to take his wife out to dinner.

Someone might say I shouldn't give gifts with strings attached — go ahead. But don't say it to God, because all of His gifts come with strings attached (See Ephesians 4:12, I Peter 4:10).

How To Be Successful

A lady was attending a reception with her husband. People were milling around talking and getting acquainted. A stranger approached her and asked her name. During the conversation, the stranger asked, "What do you do for a living?" The lady replied, "I am the Chief Operations

Officer of a small corporation." The stranger smiled and asked the type of business she ran. The lady replied, "My home. I am a housewife." She considered herself a success because she ran her home properly. As I mentioned before, "*It is not what you are that holds you back, but what you think you're not.*" I am afraid there are many who are successful but think they are not.

What is success? To some, it is reaching a certain level of financial independence. To others, it is becoming relatively famous. Still others believe that winning a certain number of souls to Christ or building their church to a certain size is success.

The really successful people are those who have found God's will and are living in it to the best of their abilities. It has been wisely said, "To know God's will is the greatest knowledge, to do God's will is the greatest achievement." *Success is being where God placed you, doing what God wants you to do with the gifts He has given you.*

One of the dangers of the success philosophy prevalent today is what I call the *Abraham Lincoln Syndrome.* So many success teachers, authors, even pastors are telling us, "Anyone can be another Abraham Lincoln (or whatever hero you choose). Abe was raised in a log cabin by a poor family. He read by candlelight and borrowed books from neighbors and friends because he was too poor to buy them. But he grew up to be one of the greatest Presidents our country has had. You too can be an Abraham Lincoln."

Although such teaching has challenged many to greater heights, the problem with that philosophy is that *not everyone can be an Abraham Lincoln.* Every four years, only one man out of 236 Million people will become President of the United States. Those are pretty strong odds, if you ask me. It is true that anyone can legally become President, but not everyone can go that far in their accomplishments. But everyone *can* be the best they can be within their capacity and capabilities. *Success is being the best that you can be.*

Be careful when someone says, "You can be anything you want to be." Consider the odds. Also recognize in many cases he is really saying, "You can be anything *I* want you to be." The truth is you can be everything you *should* be. You must learn to be content with being what God intended you to be and be a faithful steward of that which He entrusted to you.

People who feel good about themselves produce good results. Success is a state of mind. Successful people are people who feel good about themselves and accept themselves for who they are. They understand where they fit into the body of Christ. They think realistically. In I Corinthians 11:28, Christians are instructed "But let a man examine himself." In Romans 12:3 says, "Not to think of himself more highly than he ought to think; but to think soberly." Thinking soberly is thinking realistically, people being aware of their strengths and weaknesses, knowing their limitations, talents abilities and making decisions accordingly. They realize they are accountable to God for just what God has given them, no more and no less. Knowing one's spiritual gifts and functioning within those gifts is doing God's will.

Success is not just achievement, but achieving. Success must be an ongoing process, moving from one successful event to another. It is always sprinkled with failures and mistakes, but is still a continuous upward movement.

To the believer, this process is spiritual growth and maturity. The purpose of Scripture is "that the man of God may be perfect" (II Timothy 3:17). The word perfect means complete or mature. We will never be completely mature until we see Christ face to face. But we are to be continually in the process of growth, preparing for that time when we see Him.

On the side of a rolling hill, deep in a valley, nestled between two mighty Swiss mountains was a small country graveyard. In it stood many great monuments honoring the men and women who had died in the little Swiss community. But one small unnoticed gravestone read more honorably than them all — "He died climbing" — the highest honor that could be given to the dead of a town of mountain climbers and guides. He had died on his way to the top. "He died climbing" — reaching for that unreachable peak. Climbing on, day in and day out, always on the way to the top, always seeking to serve Christ to the fullest. That's the way for the Christian to be successful — achieving rather than having achieved.

Now What?

It is not enough for the believer just to learn his spiritual gift. He must utilize it and develop it. God did not give spiritual gifts as ornaments or fancy names to be pinned on His children so they could tell the world "I am a teacher", "I am a server", or "I am an exhorter". He intended them to be used in the ministry.

In order for them to be used to the fullest, there must be a continuous development process. For many years I, like many others, taught there are three phases of spiritual gifts: (1) discover or recognize; (2) develop; and (3) use the gift. I, like everyone else, was guilty of not telling people HOW to develop and not showing them HOW to use the gifts they had. Now, I realize that is not the proper procedure. The proper procedure is (1) discover or recognize; (2) use; and (3) develop. *You can develop a gift only as you use it.* A gift in itself cannot be developed. It is developed through functioning. As a believer develops and trains for an area of ministry, and functions within his spiritual gift, he is developing his gift. A year cannot be spent developing a spiritual gift before it is utilized since one gift can manifest itself in many different ministries. As the believer utilizes his gift within the framework of a given ministry, he expands the capacity, motivation and characteristics of that gift. As he develops the ministry, he develops the gift. If it could be placed in equation form, it would be: DISCOVERY + USE = DEVELOPMENT.

For example, a person with the gift of exhortation will learn more practical steps and be able to help those he teaches as he learns how his area of ministry functions best. He will attend seminars, read books, listen to tapes and take advantage of other educational opportunities concerning that particular area of ministry. By doing so, he will expand his gift of exhortation so that he can relay the practical aspects of that education to those involved with him in that ministry. The administrator will use the same process. He will learn new management techniques so that he can better function as a leader. The pastor-teacher will learn more spiritual traits from the Bible, the teacher more knowledge and facts and so on. As these people learn their ministry, they learn how to utilize their gifts more effectively.

Also a part of developing the gift is the expanding and developing of the ENABLING Gifts. Since they are the catalysts of the spiritual gifts, they will speed up the development process as they are applied to the ministry within the gifted area. They will strengthen the TEAM Gifts, expand them and enlarge the capacity. Thus the gift is developed and made more effective.

The whole idea is for God's people to recognize their spiritual gifts and spend the rest of their lives utilizing their gifts in the ministry of *reaching* and *teaching* their generation for God.

FOOTNOTES:

[1] HAUCK, Gary L., *Is My Church What God Meant It to Be?* (Accent-B/P Publications: Denver, 1979) Page 77.
[2] WAGNER, C. Peter, *Your Spiritual Gift Can Help Your Church Grow* (Regal Books: Glendale, 1979) Page 40.

CHAPTER TWELVE

REVIEW QUESTIONS:

1. What 4 things must be avoided when finding your place on the TEAM?

2. What would be the worst abuse concerning your spiritual gift and your secular employment?

3. What is the difference between vocation and avocation?

DISCUSSION QUESTIONS:

1. What is your definition of success and how do you plan to reach that point in your own life and ministry?

2. Who are the most successful people you know and why do you feel they are successful?

3. Do you consider yourself successful? Why? What needs to be done to improve?

GLOSSARY

ABRAHAM LINCOLN SYNDROME: The philosophy of success that says, "You can be an Abraham Lincoln" or some other great person. It ignores the fact that each person's gift and abilities have a certain capacity which allows only a certain level to be achieved successfully.

ADMINISTRATION, THE GIFT OF: The Spirit-given capacity and desire to serve God by organizing, administering, promoting and leading the various affairs of the church.

ANTI-CHARISMATIC: The position on miraculous gifts holding the same position as non-Charismatic, but tending to take the extreme doctrines of Charismatics and tagging *all* Charismatics with them. This position belittles and often leads to personal attacks.

BIBLICAL PROCEDURE FOR TRAINING CHRISTIANS: Based on II Timothy 3:16-17; using the Scriptures to teach doctrine (what to believe), to reprove (confront sin), to correct (showing the alternative action to sin) and to instruct in righteousness (how to live) with importance placed on the order in which they appear in verse 16.

BURDEN: A motivating force from within that makes a demand on one's resources, whether material (I Thess. 2:6) or emotional; an unsatisfiable hunger gnawing at your soul; a burning in one's heart to do what God has called him to do.

CAPACITY: Enabling for the future; may or may not be fulfilled; must be recognized and developed in the life of the believer.

CATALYST GIFTS: Another name for ENABLING gifts, because they put the tools (TEAM Gifts) and the field of service together to get the job done; also called empowering gifts.

CHARISMATIC: The position concerning miraculous gifts holding that all gifts are valid today and are given just as they were in the early church.

CHURCH GROWTH: The movement concerned with the science of church growth; its major contributing factor is methodology; the newest of six major Bible-centered church movements.

CONFRONTATIONAL EVANGELISM: The type of evangelism that compels the individual to confront every lost person he meets with the Gospel. Witnessing goes beyond personal testimony, requiring a presentation of the Gospel and pursuing a decision every time.

DIVISION OF LABOR: Principle which states, "God will not do what He has commanded you to do, and you cannot do what God has reserved as His authority or duty." Based on I Corinthians 3:9. (Towns)

EASY-BELIEVISM: When the salvation experience is explained by an emphasis on the verbal decision (faith), often at the expense of compelling the sinner to actually repent of his sinful condition.

ENABLING GIFTS: Those gifts given to every believer for the purpose of enabling him to minister to others. They develop character rather than tasks. They are faith, discernment, wisdom and knowledge.

EVANGELIST, THE GIFT OF: The Spirit-given capacity and desire to serve God by leading people beyond the natural sphere of influence to the saving knowledge of Jesus Christ; the aggressive soul-winner who seeks the lost.

EXHORTATION, THE GIFT OF: The Spirit-given capacity and desire to serve God by motivating others to action by urging them to pursue a course of conduct; the "How-to" teacher, giving the practical application of God's Word.

GIFT AWARENESS: Knowing your spiritual gift and ways it can be exercised; an awareness of others' gifts and how they can be exercised.

GIFT BLINDNESS: A condition which results from Gift Ignorance and renders the victim incapable of recognizing his own spiritual gifts and their influence upon his own life and ministry.

GIFT COLONIZATION: The direct and inescapable result of unrestrained gift gravitation; building of "colonies" of a certain gift, usually a church full of them, but extending to "movements" as well.

GIFT COVETING: The activity of desiring a gift other than that which has been given to an individual by God.

GIFT DODGING: The act of trying to dodge your responsibility that comes with your spiritual gift; ignoring the fact you have a gift and its place in God's work.

GIFT GRAVITATION: The tendency among Christians to attract and be attracted to other Christians with like spiritual gifts.

GIFT IGNORANCE: A lack of knowledge regarding the possession of spiritual gifts and their function.

GIFT IMPOSING: The act of forcing one's spiritual gift upon another and attempting to compel them to perform as though it was God's gift to them as well.

GIFT MIX: Teaches that the majority, if not all, Christians have a variety of gifts, degrees of giftedness and multiple ministries through which each gift can be exercised; mixtures of these elements give each believer his or her identity in the body of Christ. (Wagner)

GIFT OBSESSION: Allowing the matter of gifts to get out of perspective by overemphasizing them while underemphasizing other equally important areas of the ministry.

GIVING, THE GIFT OF: The Spirit-given capacity and desire to serve God by giving his material resources, far beyond the tithe, to further the work of God; the person who meets financial needs of his fellow Christians and church members.

GUILT-TRIP MOTIVATION: Compelling people to action by placing guilt on them rather than letting the Holy Spirit convict; the attitude of making others feel inferior and that they are not right with God.

HOMOGENEOUS UNIT: A church or congregation consisting of people with similar social, ethnic, racial or linguistic backgrounds. People are usually drawn to churches where they do not have to cross those barriers. (McGavran)

LAW OF FIRST EXPOSURE: The first exposure a person has to a principle or teaching is the one which dominates his beliefs about that principle or teaching regardless of what he is taught or how much he is taught thereafter.

LAW OF DIMINISHING PROSPECTS: The longer a person is a Christian, the fewer unsaved people are in his circles of concern, thus the less likelihood of him reaching new people.

LIFESTYLE EVANGELISM: A form of non-confrontational evangelism; living your life that others might see Christ in you.

LIMITED CHARISMATIC: The position that holds that all gifts are valid today but God distributes the gifts within the "Universal Church" and different gifts manifest themselves in different local assemblies of believers.

LITTLE TOE PRINCIPLE: Based on the analogy of the human body and the Body of Christ: the little toe is necessary to the human body for balance; every believer's spiritual gift is necessary to the church in order to give balance.

MERCY SHOWING, THE GIFT OF: The Spirit-given capacity and desire to serve God by identifying and comforting those who are in distress; the Christian who understands and comforts his fellow Christian; the empathizer.

MINISTERING GIFTS: The "King-makers" who work behind the scenes in support roles to the speaking gifts. (I Peter 4:9-11)

MIRACULOUS GIFTS: Often called "Charismatic Gifts" because they are accepted primarily within the Charismatic Movement. They are Apostles, Tongues, Interpretations of Tongues, Miracles and Healing.

NON-CHARISMATIC: Position that holds that all gifts are NOT valid today; miraculous gifts should not be exercised in any church today.

PASTOR-TEACHER, THE GIFT OF: The Spirit-given capacity and desire to serve God by overseeing, training and caring for the needs of a group of Christians; the shepherd who leads and feeds; the coach of the team.

PERSONAL MINISTRY: That activity which the individual Christian does for God which benefits someone else.

PROCEDURE FOR DEVELOPING METHODOLOGY: (1) The Bible as a foundation; (2) interpretation; (3) philosophy of ministry based on interpretation; (4) methodology based on the philosophy; the opposite of Theo-methodologist's approach.

PROPHECY, THE GIFT OF: The Spirit-given capacity and desire to serve God by proclaiming God's truth; the hell-fire and brimstone preacher pointing out sin.

SERVING, THE GIFT OF: The Spirit-given capacity and desire to serve God by rendering practical help in both physical and spiritual matters; the person who meets the practical needs of his fellow Christians and the church.

SPEAKING GIFTS: The division of TEAM gifts which are usually used in public or platform ministry by speaking, teaching and preaching the Word of God. (I Peter 4:9-11)

SPIRITUAL GIFT: A supernatural capacity and desire to serve God in a certain way, graciously given by a Sovereign God at the time of the new birth in order for the believer to minister to his fellow man for the purpose of accomplishing His work through the believer.

SUCCESS: Being where God placed you, doing what God wants you to do with the gifts He gave you.

TEACHER, THE GIFT OF: The person with the Spirit-given capacity and desire to serve God by making clear the truth of the Word of God with accuracy and simplicity; the scholar making clear the doctrines and teachings of the Bible.

TEAM: A group of active people empowered by the Holy Spirit and gifted in the various gifts for the purpose of meeting the needs of people.

TEAM COUNSELING: Using the various TEAM gifts to help in the process of counseling; each gift exercises its own special ability to meet the need of the counselee, such as the prophet confronting sin, the exhorter giving practical "how to" or the mercy shower giving sympathy and comfort.

TEAM EVANGELISM: Using all the spiritual gifts in a team effort to bring people to Christ. Uses lifestyle coupled with confrontation in order to reach a person for Christ.

TEAM GIFTS: Also called "task oriented gifts" because they are functions rather than character qualities; a possessed quality; they function in the actual ministry to meet needs. They are Evangelist, Prophet, Teacher, Exhortation, Pastor-teacher, Showing Mercy, Serving, Giving and Administration.

TEAM MINISTRY: A philosophy of ministry centered on the believer; holds that every Christian has a spiritual gift and therefore has a responsibility to function as part of the team; the gifts will govern the ministry's direction and thrust; people centered rather than task centered.

THEO-METHODOLOGIST: The person whose methods have become his theology, usually because the methods work; scripturalizes the methodology rather than building methodology and philosophy on doctrine and Scripture (see Procedure for Developing Methodology).

WORKFORCE ECONOMICS: The act of using people where they are usable; putting gifted people where their gifts are best utilized to do God's work.

BIBLIOGRAPHY

Arn, Charles, McGavran, Donald and Arn, Win. *Growth A New Vision for the Sunday School*. Pasadena, CA: Church Growth Press, 1980.

Arn, Win (edited by). *The Pastor's Church Growth Handbook, Volume I*. Pasadena, CA: Church Growth Press, 1979.

---------- (edited by). *The Pastor's Church Growth Handbook, Volume II*. Pasadena, CA: Church Growth Press, 1982.

Arthur, Kay. *How to Discover Your Spiritual Gifts*. Chattanooga, TN: Reach Out, Inc., 1977.

Bennett, Dennis and Rita. *The Holy Spirit and You*. Plainfield, NJ: Logos International, 1971.

Bittlinger, Arnold. *Gifts and Graces*. Grand Rapids, MI: William B. Eerdmans Publishing Company, 1967.

Blanchard, Tim. *A Practical Guide to Finding Your Spiritual Gifts*. Wheaton, IL: Tyndale House Publishers, Inc., 1979.

Bridge, Donald and Phypers, David. *Spiritual Gifts & The Church*. Downers Grove,, IL: InterVarsity Press, 1973.

Brown, Woodrow (edited by). *The Person and Work of the Holy Spirit*. Bible School Park, NY: Echoes Publishing Company, 1948. (By senior students of the classes of 1947 and 1948 as taught by Rev. H. H. Wagner, D.D., in the Systematic Theology course at the Practical Bible Training School, Bible School Park, Broome County, NY. Editor Woodrow Brown was President of the class of 1948.)

Bullinger, E. W. *The Giver and His Gifts*. Grand Rapids, MI: Kregel Publications, 1905.

Carter, Howard. *Spiritual Gifts and Their Operation*. Springfield, MO: Gospel Publishing House, 1968.

Charles E. Fuller Institute. *Spiritual Gifts & Church Growth Leader's Guide*. Pasadena, CA: Charles E. Fuller Institute, 1978.

Christenson, Larry. *Speaking In Tongues*. Minneapolis, MN: Dimension Books, 1968.

---------- *The Gift of Tongues*. Minneapolis, MN: Bethany Fellowship, Inc., 1963.

Clark, Martin E. *Choosing Your Career: The Christian's Decision Manual.* Phillipsburg, NJ: Presbyterian and Reformed Publishing Company, 1981.

Clark, Steve. *Baptized in the Spirit and Spiritual Gifts.* Pecos, NM: Dove Publications, 1969.

Clayton, Lynn P. *No Second-Class Christians.* Nashville, TN: Broadman Press, 1976.

Clinton, Bobby. *Spirtual Gifts.* Coral Gables, FL: Learning Resource Center Publications, 1975.

Criswell, W.A. *The Baptism, Filling & Gifts of the Holy Spirit.* Grand Rapids, MI: Zondervan Publishing House, 1973.

----------. *The Holy Spirit in Today's World.* Grand Rapids, MI: Zondervan Publishing House, 1966.

Cumming, James Elder. *A Handbook on The Holy Spirit.* Minneapolis, MN: Dimension Books, 1965.

Dale, Robert D. *To Dream Again.* Nashville, TN: Broadman Press, 1981.

David C. Cook Publishing Co. *Congratulations-You're Gifted.* Elgin, IL: David C. Cook Publishing Co., 1975.

Dillon, William S. *God's Work in God's Way.* Woodworth, WI: Brown Gold Publications, 1957.

Dollar, George W., Ph.D. *The New Testament and New Pentecostalism.* Maple Grove, MN: Nystrom Publishing Company, 1978.

Edwards, Gene. *How to Have a Soul Winning Church.* Springfield, MO: Gospel Publishing House, 1962.

Engstrom, Ted W. *Your Gift of Administration How to Discover and Use It.* Nashville, TN: Thomas Nelson Publishers, 1979.

Epp, Theodore H. *Spiritual Gifts for Every Believer.* Lincoln, NE: Back to the Bible, 1962.

Falwell, Jerry, Ed Dobson, and Ed Hindson, editors. *The Fundamentalist Phenomenon.* Garden City, NY: Doubleday and Company, Inc., 1981.

Falwell, Jerry and Towns, Elmer. *Stepping Out On Faith.* Wheaton, IL: Tyndale House Publishers, Inc., 1984.

Felker, Lenoir M. *The Fruit and Gifts of the Holy Spirt Teacher's Manual.* Marion, IN: The Wesley Press, 1979.

Finney, Charles G. (Complied and edited by Timothy L. Smith.) *The Promise of The Spirit.* Minneapolis, MN: Bethany House Publishers, 1980.

Fisk, Samuel. *Divine Healing Under the Searchlight.* Schaumburg, IL: Regular Baptist Press, 1978.

Flynn, Leslie B. *19 Gifts of The Spirit.* Wheaton, IL: Victor Books, 1974.

Frost, Robert C., Ph.D. *Aglow with The Spirit.* Plainfield, NJ: Logas International, 1965.

Gangel, Kenneth O. *You and Your Spiritual Gifts.* Chicago, IL: Moody Press, 1975.

----------. *Unwrap Your Spiritual Gifts.* Wheaton, IL: Victor Books, 1983.

Gardiner, George E. *The Corinthian Catastrophe.* Grand Rapids, MI: Kregel Publications, 1974.

Gee, Donald. *Concerning Spiritual Gifts.* Springfield, MO: Radiant Books, 1949.

----------. *Spiritual Gifts in the Work of the Ministry Today.* Springfield, MO: Gospel Publishing House, 1963.

----------. *Toward Pentecostal Unity.* Springfield, MO: Gospel Publishing House, 1961.

Gillquist, Peter E. *Let's Quit Fighting About The Holy Spirit.* Grand Rapids, MI: Zondervan Publishing House, 1974.

Gordon, A.J. *The Ministry of The Spirit.* Minneapolis, MN: Bethany Fellowship, Inc., 1964.

Gower, David M. *Questions of the Charismatics.* Schaumburg, IL: Regular Baptist Press, 1981.

Graham, Billy. *The Holy Spirit Activating God's Power In Your Life.* Waco, TX: Word Books, 1978.

Griffiths, Michael. *Grace-Gifts.* Grand Rapids, MI: William B. Eerdmans Publishing Company, 1978.

Hagin, Kenneth E. *Seven Vital Steps to Receiving The Holy Spirit.* Tulsa, OK: Kenneth Hagin Ministries, Inc., 1980.

----------. *Concerning Spiritual Gifts.* Tulsa, OK: Kenneth Hagin Ministries, Inc., 1974.

Hauck, Gary L. *Is My Church What God Meant It to Be.* Denver, CO: Accent B/P Publications, 1979.

Hendrix, John D. *Nexus.* Nashville, TN: Convention Press, 1974.

Hickey, Marilyn, *Seven Gifts To Success.* Denver, CO: Life for Laymen, Inc.1976.

Hocking, David L. *Spiritual Gifts.* Sounds of Grace Ministries, 1975.

Horton, Harold. *The Gifts of The Spirit.* Springfield, MO: Gospel Publishing House, 1934.

Hubbard, David Allan. *Unwrapping The Gifts of God.* Pasadena, CA: Fuller Evangelistic Association, 1983.

Hurn, Raymond W., Dr. *Finding Your Ministry.* Kansas City, MO: Beacon Hill Press of Kansas City, 1979.

----------. *Spiritual Gifts Workshop.* Kansas City, MO: Department of Home Missions, 1978.

Hutchins, Clair Dean and Gibson, Brother John. *Winning the World.* St. Petersburg, FL: World Mission Crusade, 1985.

Hutson, Curtis, Dr. *The Fullness of the Holy Spirit.* Murfreesboro, TN: Sword of The Lord Publishers, 1981.

Hyles, Jack, Dr. *Meet The Holy Spirit.* Hammond, IN: Hyles-Anderson Publishers, 1982.

Innes, Dick. *I Hate Witnessing.* Ventura, CA: Vision House, 1983.

Institute For American Church Growth. *How to Mobilize Your Laity for Ministry Through Your Church.* Pasadena, CA: Institute for American Church Growth.

----------. *Spiritual Gifts for Building the Body.* Pasadena, CA: Institute for American Church Growth, 1979.

Ironside, H.A. *The Mission of The Holy Spirit and Praying in The Holy Spirit.* Neptune, NJ: Loizeaux Brothers, 1957.

Jowett, J. H. *Life in the Heights.* Grand Rapids, MI: Baker Book House, 1925.

Judisch, Douglas. *An Evaluation of Claims to the Charismatic Gifts.* Grand Rapids, MI: Baker Book House, 1978.

Kilinski, Kenneth K. and Wofford, Jerry C. *Organization and Leadership in the Local Church*. Grand Rapids, MI: Zondervan Publishing House, 1973.

Kinghorn, Kenneth Cain. *Gifts of the Spirit*. Nashville, TN: Abingdon Press, 1976.

----------. *Discovering Your Spiritual Gifts: A Personal Method*. Wilmore, KY: Francis Asbury Publishing Company, Inc., 1981.

Koch, Kurt. *Charismatic Gifts*. Quebec, Canada: The Association for Christian Evangelism (Quebec) Inc., 1975.

----------. *The Strife of Tongues*. Grand Rapids, MI: Kregel Publications, 1969.

Kuyper, Abraham, D.D., LL.D., (translated from the Dutch with Explanatory Notes by Rev. Henri De Vries). *The Work of The Holy Spirit*. Grand Rapids, MI: Wm. B. Eerdmans Publishing Co., 1900.

LeTourneau, R.G. *Mover of Men and Mountains*. Chicago, IL: Moody Press, 1960.

Lightner, Robert P. *Speaking in Tongues and Divine Healing*. Schaumburg, IL: Regular Baptist Press, 1965.

Lovett, C.S. *Witnessing Made Easy*. Baldwin Park, CA: Personal Christianity, 1964.

MacArthur, John F., Jr. *The Charismatics: A Doctrinal Perspective*. Grand Rapids, MI: Zondervan Publishing House, 1978.

----------. *Keys To Spiritual Growth*. Old Tappan, NJ: Fleming H. Revell Company, 1976.

MacGorman, J. W. *The Gifts of The Spirit*. Nashville, TN: Broadman Press, 1974.

Martin, Paul. *The Holy Spirit Today*. Kansas City, MO: Beacon Hill Press of Kansas City, 1970.

Mattson, Ralph and Miller, Arthur. *Finding a Job You Can Love*. Nashville, TN: Thomas Nelson Publishers, 1982.

Maxwell, John C., Dr. *Biblically Teaching Spiritual Gifts*. San Diego, CA:

---------- and Reiland, Dan M. *A Practical Guide to Lay Involvement in Your Church*. Lemon Grove, CA: Skyline Wesleyan Church, 1983.

McGee, J. Vernon. *I Corinthians*. Pasadena, CA: Thru The Bible Books, 1977.

----------. *Ephesians.* Pasadena, CA: Thru The Bible Books, 1977.

----------. *Talking in Tongues!* Pasadena, CA: Thru The Bible Books, 1963.

----------. *Gifts of The Spirit.* Pasadena, CA: Thru The Bible Books, 1979.

McMinn, Gordon N., Ph.D. *Spiritual Gifts Inventory.* Portland, OR: Western Baptist Press, 1978.

McNair, Jim. *Experiencing The Holy Spirit.* Minneapolis, MN: Bethany Fellowship, Inc., 1977.

McRae, William J. *The Dynamics of Spiritual Gifts.* Grand Rapids, MI: Zondervan Publishing House, 1976.

Miller, Arthur F. and Mattson, Ralph T. *The Truth about You.* Old Tappan, NJ: Fleming H. Revell Company, 1977.

Miller, Basil. *George Muller Man of Faith & Miracles.* Minneapolis, MN: Dimension Books, 1941.

Mundell, George H. *The Ministry of The Holy Spirit.* Darby, PA: Maranantha Publications, date unknown.

Murray, Andrew (edited by). *The Power of The Spirit: Selections from the Writings of William Law.* Minneapolis, MN: Dimension Books, 1977.

Neighbour, Ralph W., Jr. *This Gift is Mine.* Nashville, TN: Broadman Press, 1974.

Nystrom, Carolyn. *The Holy Spirit in Me.* Chicago, IL: Moody Press, 1980.

O'Conner, Elizabeth. *Eighth Day of Creation.* Waco, TX: Word Books, 1971.

Owen, John, D.D. *The Holy Spirit His Gifts and Power.* Grand Rapids, MI: Kregel Publications, 1954.

Pache, Rene (Translated by J. D. Emerson, Vennessur Lausanne). *The Person and Work of The Holy Spirit.* Chicago, IL: Moody Press, 1954.

Palmer, John M. *Equipping for Ministry.* Springfield, MO: Gosppel Publishing House, 1985.

Pearlman, Myer. *Let's Meet The Holy Spirit.* Springfield, MO: Gospel Publishing House, 1935.

Picirilli, Robert E. *The Gifts of The Spirit.* Nashville, TN: Randall House Publications, 1980.

Pickering, Ernest, Dr. *Charismatic Confusion*. Schaumburg, IL: Regular Baptist Press, 1976.

Prange, Erwin E. *The Gift Is Already Yours*. Minneapolis, MN: Bethany Fellowship, Inc., 1980.

Purkiser, W.T. *The Gifts of The Spirit*. Kansas City, MO: Beacon Hill Press of Kansas City, 1975.

Rea, John, Editor with several contributing editors. *The Layman's Commentary on The Holy Spirit*. Plainfield, NJ: Logos International, 1972.

Reeves, R. Daniel and Jenson, Ronald. *Always Advancing: Modern Strategies for Church Growth*. San Bernardino, CA: Here's Life Publishers, Inc., 1984.

Rice, John R., Dr. *The Charismatic Movement*. Murfreesboro, TN: Sword of The Lord Publishers, 1976.

----------. *How Jesus, Our Pattern, Was Filled With The Holy Spirit*. Murfreesboro, TN: Sword of The Lord Publishers, 1946.

----------. *How Great Soul Winners Were Filled With The Holy Spirit*. Murfreesboro, TN: Sword of The Lord Publishers, 1949.

----------. *The Fullness of The Spirit*. Murfreesboro, TN: Sword of The Lord Publishers, 1946.

----------. *The Christian and The Holy Spirit*. Murfreesboro, TN: Sword of The Lord Publishers, 1972.

Ridenhour, Lynn. *Spirit Aflame: An Autobiography*. St. Paul, MN: Braun Press, 1980.

Robison, James. *New Growth: What The Holy Spirit Wants to do for You*. Wheaton, IL: Tyndale House, 1978.

Ryrie, Charles Caldwell. *The Holy Spirit*. Chicago, IL: Moody Press, 1965.

Schlink, Basilea. *Ruled by The Spirit*. Minneapolis, MN: Dimension Books, 1969.

Schuller, Robert H. *Self Esteem: The New Reformation*. Waco, TX: Word Books, 1982.

Senter, Mark, III. *The Art of Recruiting Volunteers*. Wheaton, IL: Victor Books, 1960.

Settel, T. S. (edited by). *The Faith of Billy Graham*. New York, NY: The New American Library, Inc., 1968.

Smith, Charles R. *Tongues in Biblical Perspective.* Winona Lake, IN: BMH Books, 1972.

Stanger, F.B. *The Gifts of the Spirit.* Harrisburg, PA: Christian Publications Inc.,1974.

Stedman, Ray C. *Body Life.* Glendale, CA: Regal Books, 1972.

----------. *A Study Guide for Body Life.* Glendale, CA: Regal Books, 1977.

Swindoll, Charles R. *Tongues: An Answer to Charismatic Confusion.* Portland, OR: Multnomah Press, 1981.

Synan, Vinson, Editor. *Aspects of Pentecostal-Charismatic Origins.* Plainfield, NJ: Logos International, 1975.

Taylor, Jack R. *After The Spirit Comes. . ..* Nashville, TN: Broadman Press, 1974.

The Sunday School Board of the Southern Baptist Convention. *Discovering Your Spiritual Gifts.* Nashville, TN: The Sunday School Board of the Southern Baptist Convention, 1981.

Thomas, Robert L. *Understanding Spiritual Gifts.* Chicago, IL: Moody Press, 1978.

Torrey, R.A. *The Baptism with the Holy Spirit.* Minneapolis, MN: Dimension Books, 1972.

----------. *How to Find Fullness of Power in Christian Life and Service.* Minneapolis, MN: Bethany House Publishers, 1903.

Tournier, Paul. *The Meaning of Gifts.* Atlanta, GA: John Knox Press, 1961.

Towns, Elmer. *A Fresh Start in Life Now That You Are a Christian.* Roanoke, VA: Progress Press, Inc., 1976.

----------. *What the Faith Is All About.* Wheaton, IL: Tyndale House Publishers, Inc., 1983.

----------. *What the Faith Is All About: Leader's Guide.* Wheaton, IL: Tyndale House Publishers, Inc., 1984.

----------. *Say-It-Faith.* Wheaton, IL: Tyndale House Publishers, Inc., 1983.

Tozer, A.W. *Tragedy in the Church: The Missing Gifts.* Harrisburg, PA: Christian Publications, Inc., 1978.

Unger, Merrill F. *The Baptism & Gifts of the Holy Spirit.* Chicago, IL: Moody Press, 1974.

Van Der Puy, Abe C. *The High Calling of God: You can Serve Successfully.* Lincoln, NE: Back to the Bible, 1982.

Vaughan, C.R., D.D. *The Gifts of The Holy Spirit.* Carlisle, PA: The Banner of Truth Trust, 1894.

Wagner, C. Peter. *Your Spiritual Gifts Can Help Your Church Grow.* Glendale, CA: Regal Books, 1979.

----------. *Your Church Can Grow.* Glendale, CA: Regal Books, 1976.

----------. *Your Church Can Be Healthy.* Nashville, TN: Abingdon, 1979.

Walvoord, John F., A.M., Th.D. *The Holy Spirit.* Grand Rapids, MI: Zondervan Publishing House, 1954.

Watts, Wayne. *The Gift of Giving.* Colorado Springs, CO: Navpress, 1982.

Webley, Simon. *How to Give Away Your Money.* Downers Grove, IL: InterVarsity Press, 1978.

Wemp, C. Sumner. *How on Earth Can I Be Spiritual?* Nashville, TN: Thomas Nelson Inc., Publishers, 1978.

Wesley, John as paraphrased by Clare Weakley. *The Holy Spirit and Power.* Plainfield, NJ: Logos International, 1977.

Williams, John. *The Holy Spirit, Lord and Life-Giver.* Neptune, NJ: Loizeaux Brothers, 1928.

----------. *The Holy Spirit, Lord and Life-Giver Study Guide.* Neptune, NJ: Loizeaux Brothers, 1980.

Willmington, Harold. *The Doctrine of the Holy Spirit.* Lynchburg, VA: personal publication.

Winslow, Octavius. *The Work of The Holy Spirit.* Carlisle, PA: The Banner of Truth Trust, 1840.

Yocum, Bruce. *Prophecy: Exercising the Prophetic Gifts of the Spirit in the Church Today.* Ann Arbor, MI: Servant Books, 1976.

Yohn, Rick. *Discover Your Spiritual Gift and Use It.* Wheaton, IL: Tyndale House Publishers, Inc., 1974.

Zeller, George W. *God's Gift of Tongues.* Neptune, NJ: Loizeaux Brothers, 1978.

Recognizing that it takes a TEAM to build any work for God, we salute **our** TEAM at Church Growth Institute who helped in the production, printing, shipping and other work of getting this material into your hands. Each was not only faithful in using his or her spiritual gift, but in giving 100% to the task that was assigned. A big THANKS to each of them.

Double Your Lay Involvement With
TEAM MINISTRY

A Resource Packet is Available for Teachers and Leaders to teach the principles of this textbook in your church

---

The Team Ministry Resource Packet has two complete manuals.

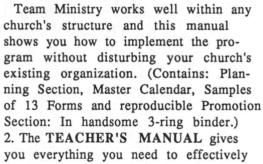

1. The **IMPLEMENTATION MANUAL** is designed so the pastor need only launch the program. After that the manual provides everything he needs for a continuing lay involvement ministry.

Team Ministry works well within any church's structure and this manual shows you how to implement the program without disturbing your church's existing organization. (Contains: Planning Section, Master Calendar, Samples of 13 Forms and reproducible Promotion Section: In handsome 3-ring binder.)

2. The **TEACHER'S MANUAL** gives you everything you need to effectively teach the principles of spiritual gifts and lay involvement to your people. It can be adapted to any preaching service, a three hour workshop, an eight hour seminar, Sunday School, training hour or home Bible study. (Contains: Preparation Section, Visual Aids, Leader's Workbook and three Cassettes; In 3-ring vinyl binder.)

Team Ministry Resource packet..................................only $79.95

Spiritual Gifts Inventory

This is the best test available anywhere to help you "Discover" your spiritual gifts. Inventory can be taken in 20 to 30 minutes by the average reader. Answer sheet is self scoring. Gives an instant profile and bar graph.
Questionnaire and Answer Sheet sold separately.

1-9 copies..................$1.00 each
10-49 copies...............$ .75 each
50-99 copies...............$ .50 each
100 or more...............$ .40 each

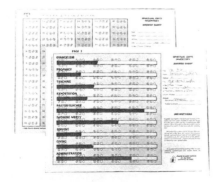

ORDER FORM

Please allow three (3) weeks from receipt of order for delivery.

Please send the following items:

_____ Team Ministry Resource Packet at $79.95 each................................ $ _____

_____ Spiritual Gifts Inventory Answer Sheets at $_____ each................. $ _____

_____ Spiritual Gifts Inventory Questionnaires at $_____ each................ $ _____

Total $ _____

Shipping _____ $2.50 _____

Amount
Enclosed _____

Name _____ Position _____

Church _____

Address _____

City _____ State _____ Zip _____

Send orders to: *Church Growth Institute*
                   P.O. BOX 4404, Lynchburg, VA 24502

Orders under $25.00 must be prepaid.

ORDER FORM

Please allow three (3) weeks from receipt of order for delivery.

Please send the following items:

_____ Team Ministry Resource Packet at $79.95 each . . . . $_____

_____ Spiritual Gifts Inventory Answer Sheets at $_____ each . . . . $_____

_____ Spiritual Gifts Inventory Questionnaires at $_____ each . . . . $_____

Total $_____

Shipping _____ $2.50

Amount
Enclosed _____

Orders under $25.00 must be prepaid.

Name _____ Position _____

Church _____

Address _____

City _____ State _____ Zip _____

Send orders to: *Church Growth Institute*
                  P.O. Box 4404, Lynchburg, VA 24502

ORDER FORM

Please allow three (3) weeks from receipt of order for delivery.

Please send the following items:

_____ Team Ministry Resource Packet at $79.95 each . . . . $ _____

_____ Spiritual Gifts Inventory Answer Sheets at $ _____ each . . . . $ _____

_____ Spiritual Gifts Inventory Questionnaires at $ _____ each . . . . $ _____

Total $ _____

Shipping _____$2.50_____

Amount
Enclosed _____

Name _____ Position _____

Church _____

Address _____

City _____ State _____ Zip _____

Send orders to: **Church Growth Institute**
P.O. Box 4404, Lynchburg, VA 24502

Orders under $25.00 must be prepaid.